Afterthoughts on
Material Civilization
and Capitalism

The Johns Hopkins Symposia in Comparative History

The Johns Hopkins Symposia in Comparative History are occasional volumes sponsored by the Department of History at The Johns Hopkins University and The Johns Hopkins University Press, comprising original essays by leading scholars in the United States and other countries. Each volume considers, from a comparative perspective, an important topic of current historical interest. The present volume is the seventh. Its preparation has been assisted by the Phillip W. Haberman, Jr., Foundation.

Fernand Braudel

Afterthoughts on
Material Civilization
and Capitalism

Translated by Patricia M. Ranum

THE JOHNS HOPKINS UNIVERSITY PRESS
Baltimore and London

The Johns Hopkins University Press, Baltimore, Maryland 21218
The Johns Hopkins Press Ltd., London

Library of Congress Catalog Card Number 76-47368
ISBN 0-8018-1901-6 (hardcover)
ISBN 0-8018-2217-3 (paperback)

Originally published, 1977
Johns Hopkins paperback edition, 1979

Library of Congress Cataloging in Publication data will be found on the last
printed page of this book.

Contents

Foreword   ix

I.   Afterthoughts on Material Life   3

II.   The Market Economy and Capitalism   39

III. Capitalism and Dividing Up the World   79

Sources of Illustrations   119

Foreword

When did Fernand Braudel first arrive at Johns Hopkins? The answer to this question may be found in and through the decades of graduate seminars taught by his good friend Frederic Chapin Lane. The Mediterranean, especially as perceived through the study of Venetian trade during the Renaissance, has been an active subject of research since Lane's arrival at Hopkins in the late 1920s. In the years following the first appearance of Braudel's *La Méditerranée et le monde méditerranéen à l'époque de Philippe II* in 1949, the library copy at Hopkins grew ragged from use—and all this well before the appearance of a second edition in 1966, the English translation in 1972, and recognition of the work as a classic of twentieth-century historical scholarship.

In the plans for the celebration of The Johns Hopkins University Centennial begun in 1974, one of the first projects proposed in the history department was an invitation to Fernand and Paule Braudel. But would they come? A gift by Mrs. Phillip W. Haberman, Jr., in memory of her husband enabled the department to extend an invitation to the Braudels. They accepted, and it was quickly agreed that the Phillip W. Haberman, Jr., lectures would focus upon Fernand Braudel's most recently completed work: a history of material civilization and capitalism, 1400–1800.

Those who shared the personal warmth and immense intellectual excitement of being with the Braudels during their visit to Baltimore in April 1976 will recall that sense of learned freedom of thought about the past conveyed in these lectures. They are afterthoughts, a summing up, an accounting of the man and his work. Fernand Braudel admitted from the start that he finds it impossible to "read" lectures, and true to this confession he spoke while scarcely looking at the texts before him. A great teacher, he would occasionally jump up to draw a graph or sketch on the blackboard to make his argument still more emphatic and specific. His auditors were swept up into a Braudelian historical world where the fruits of decades of research and daring analysis seemed to fall effortlessly and convincingly together, as he summarized and reflected upon the themes contained in his three-volume *Civilization materielle et capitalisme, 1400–1800.*

The lectures were photographed on videotape, and the Department of History hopes to be able to lend them free of charge to other universities. Every possible effort has been made to preserve in the written text the relaxed liveliness and engaging style of the original spoken French. Thanks to the translation prepared and stenciled by Patricia M. Ranum, the listeners followed the French with an English text before them. A final thank you also goes to her.

Panat   Orest Ranum
August 1976

Afterthoughts on
Material Civilization
and Capitalism

 Afterthoughts
on Material
Life

I first began thinking about this lengthy and bold undertaking many years ago, in 1950. At that time the subject was proposed to me—or, to be more accurate, imposed upon me—by Lucien Febvre, who had just begun planning a series of general historical works, *Destins du Monde* (the very series I was given the difficult task of continuing after the death of its editor in 1956). Lucien Febvre himself planned to write *Western Thought and Belief, 1400–1800* as a companion piece that was to accompany and complete my own book. Unfortunately, his book will never be published. My own work has thus been irrevocably deprived of this extra dimension.

Yet, even though it is limited chiefly to economic history, *Civilisation matérielle et capitalisme** has posed many problems for me. There has been a vast amount of documentation to absorb; the subject arouses controversy; and difficulties are constantly being created by a continually evolving historiography that must incorporate the other social sciences, albeit slowly and at times begrudgingly. This historiography, which is constantly giving birth and which is never the same from one year to the next, can only be kept up with at a run and at the cost of neglecting our routine tasks and of adapting ourselves, for better or for worse, to constantly changing demands and temptations. I, for one, have been only too happy to heed the sirens' call. And so the years have passed. I have despaired of ever reaching the harbor. I spent twenty-five years on *La Méditerraneé* and almost as many on *Civilisation matérielle et capitalisme*. No doubt that is much too long.

Economic history—a field still being developed—runs headlong into prejudices. It is not noble or magisterial, that is, exalted, history. Noble history is the ship that Lucien Febvre was building, not out of Jakob Fugger, but out of Martin Luther and François Rabelais. Noble or not, or less magisterial

---

**Civilisation matérielle et capitalisme*, 1400–1800, will comprise three volumes. The first volume is available in an English translation by Miriam Kochan, *Capitalism and Material Life*, 1400–1800 (New York, 1973). Volumes 2 and 3 will appear in 1977-78.—Trans.

than other forms of history, economic history nonetheless involves all the problems inherent in the historian's craft, it is man's entire history seen from one
particular point of view. It is both the history of those
whom we consider major actors—Jacques Coeur or
John Law—and the history of great events. It is a
history of "conjunctures"* and economic crises, and
it is the vast and structural history that evolves over
many, many years. Indeed, that is the whole problem,
for when dealing with the entire world over four
centuries, how does one organize such a file of facts
and explanations? One has to choose. I chose to deal
with long-term equilibriums and disequilibriums. To
my mind, the fundamental characteristic of the pre-
industrial economy is the coexistence of the inflexibil-
ity, inertia, and slow motion characteristic of an
economy that was still primitive, alongside
trends—limited and in the minority, yet active and
powerful—that were characteristic of modern
growth. On the one hand, peasants lived in their
villages in an almost autonomous way, virtually in an
autarchy; on the other hand, a market-oriented economy and an expanding capitalism began to spread out,
gradually creating the very world in which we live,
and, at that early date, prefiguring our world. Thus

*For a discussion of this term, see Sian Reynolds' translation of the
author's *The Mediterranean and the Mediterranean World in the Age of Phillip II*
(New York, 1975), 2: 892–900.—Trans.

we have two universes, two ways of life foreign to each other, yet whose respective wholes explain one another.

I wanted to begin with inertias—at first glance a rather indefinite sort of history that goes back beyond the clear awareness of man, who in this game is more acted upon than actor. This is what I attempted to explain in the first volume of my work, which appeared in 1967; the title page of the English edition of 1973 omitted the subtitle—"The Possible and the Impossible: Men Face to Face with Their Daily Life." I think I should really have called it "Structures of Daily Life." But that is not important. The aim of my research was clear, although the research itself proved to be unpredictable and full of blank spots, traps, and potential misinterpretations. Indeed, all the key words I used—*structure, unconscious, day-to-day-ness, depth*—are themselves indefinite. And I am not referring to the "unconscious" of psychoanalysis, although this form of unconsciousness is also involved and although the sort of collective unconsciousness whose existence caused such torment to Carl Gustav Jung needs to be defined, discovered, and pieced out. But this extremely vast subject is rarely tackled in anything but bits and pieces. It is still awaiting its historian.

I restricted myself to tangible criteria. I began with daily life, with those aspects of life that control us without our even being aware of them: habit or, better yet, routine—those thousands of acts that flower and reach fruition without anyone's having made a decision, acts of which we are not even fully aware. I think mankind is more than waist-deep in daily routine. Countless inherited acts, accumulated pell-mell and repeated time after time to this very day, become habits that help us live, imprison us, and make decisions for us throughout our lives. These acts are incentives, pulsions, patterns, ways of acting and reacting that sometimes—more frequently than we might suspect—go back to the beginnings of mankind's history. Ancient, yet still alive, this multicenturied past flows into the present like the Amazon River pouring into the Atlantic Ocean the vast flood of its cloudy waters.

I attempted to capture all this under the convenient, but inaccurate—all words with too broad a meaning are inaccurate—heading "material life." Of course, this is only one aspect of man's active life, for he is as profoundly innovative as he is enslaved by habit. At the beginning of my search, I was not concerned with delimiting where this life that is undergone rather than lived predominated, and where it disappeared. I wanted to see and to make others see this generally poorly perceived mass of indifferently lived history. I wanted to immerse myself in it and become familiar with it. Later, and only later, the time would come for me to emerge from the water. Immediately after finishing a scuba-diving expedition of this sort, the diver has the profound impression that he has been in ancient waters, probing about in the midst of a history that is, in a sense, ageless, a history that he could just as well have encountered two, three, or even ten centuries earlier and that he sometimes catches brief glimpses of here in the twentieth century. This material life as I understand it is the life that man throughout the course of his previous history has made a part of his very being, has in some way absorbed into his entrails, turning the experiments and exhilarating experiences of the past into everyday, banal necessities. So no one pays close attention to them any more.

I

This is the theme of the chapters of my first volume. The chapter titles speak for themselves, an enumeration of the vague forces that worked and pushed the whole of material life forward, and, beyond or above material life, the entire history of mankind.

The first chapter is entitled "Weight of Numbers." Biological urging in its truest form impelled man to reproduce like every other living creature—the spring tropism, as Georges Lefebvre used to call it. But there are other tropisms, other determinisms. This humanity in perpetual motion controls a good share of the destiny of mankind, although individuals themselves may be unaware of it. Given certain general conditions, according to the resources available to them, and the amount of work to be done, men became too numerous, or not numerous enough; the demographic mechanism attempted to remain balanced, but equilibrium was rarely achieved. After 1450 the number of people in Europe increased rapidly, for after the Black Death mankind was forced, and was able, to compensate for the huge losses of life during the preceding century. This recuperation continued until the next great ebbing. Following one upon the other as if planned —or so it seems to historians—these ebbs and flows reveal the rules for the long-term trends that continued to operate until the eighteenth century. Not before the eighteenth century were the frontiers of the impossible crossed and the hitherto unsurpassable population ceiling exceeded. Since then, the population has constantly increased, without a pause or a reverse in the climb. Could such a reversal possibly occur in the future?

Until the eighteenth century, the population was enclosed within an almost intangible circle. Whenever it expanded as far as the circumference, it would almost immediately pull up short and then withdraw. Ways and opportunities for restoring the balance were not lacking: penury, scarcity, famine, difficult living conditions day in and day out, war, and lastly—and above all—a constant stream of diseases. These diseases are still encountered today, but yesterday they were apocalyptic scourges: plague, which regularly swept Europe in epidemic proportions until the eighteenth century; typhus, which joined forces with winter to paralyze Napoleon and his army deep in Russia; typhoid and smallpox, which were endemic; tuberculosis, which appeared at an early date in rural areas and by the nineteenth century had swept through the cities, becoming the romantic illness *par excellence*; and venereal diseases, especially syphilis, which was reborn—or, to be more accurate, which exploded when varieties of the microbe combined—after the discovery of America. Poor hygiene and contaminated drinking water did the rest.

How could mankind, so fragile from the moment of birth, escape all these onslaughts? Infant mortality was enormous, as in certain underdeveloped countries today or yesterday, and health in general was precarious. Hundreds of autopsy records have survived, going back to the sixteenth century. They are terrifying. These descriptions of malformations, wasting illnesses, skin ailments, and abnormally large colonies of parasites in lungs and intestines would astonish a twentieth-century physician. Thus, until recent times man's history has implacably been governed by poor health conditions. We must keep this in mind when we ask: How many people were there? What illnesses did they have? Could they avoid these misfortunes?

Other questions raised by subsequent chapters of *Material Life* include: What did people eat? What did they drink? How did they dress? What were their houses like? Incongruous questions, for *homo historicus* neither eats or drinks. Yet, long ago someone said, *"Der Mensch ist was er isst,"* "Man is what he eats." Maybe it was said chiefly for the pleasure of the pun made possible by German syntax. Yet I do not think we should consider the appearance of a great number of foodstuffs as mere anecdotal history. Sugar, coffee, tea, and alcohol have each had a long-term and very important influence upon history. In any event, it is impossible to exaggerate the enormous importance of cereals, the main plants that provided food in the past. Wheat, rice, and corn represent three definitive choices made very long ago. The predominance of one grain in a civilization is the result of a countless succession of experiments that, as a result of "drifts" over a period of many centuries (to use the expression of Pierre Gourou, France's greatest geographer), gradually eliminated all other alternatives.

Europe chose wheat, which devours the soil and forces it to rest regularly; this choice implied and permitted the raising of livestock. Now, who can imagine the history of Europe without oxen, horses, plows, and carts? As a result of this choice Europe has always combined agriculture and animal husbandry. It has always been carnivorous. Rice developed out of a form of gardening, an intensive cultivation in which man could allow no room for animals. This explains why meat constitutes such a small part of the diet in rice-growing areas. Planting corn is surely the simplest and most convenient way to obtain one's "daily bread." It grows very rapidly and requires minimal care. The choice of corn as a crop left free time, making possible the forced peasant labor and the enormous monuments of the Amerindians. Society appropriated a labor force that worked the land only intermittently.

We might also discuss the number of calories that these plants represent, and inadequacies and changes in diet across the ages. Aren't these questions just as exciting as the fate of Charles V's empire or the fleeting and debatable splendors of the so-called French primacy during the reign of Louis XIV? And they are surely questions with far-reaching implications: Can't the history of the old drugs, alcohol and tobacco, and the lightning-swift manner in which tobacco in particular circled the globe and conquered the world, serve as a warning about today's drugs, different but equally dangerous?

Similar observations apply to technical skills. Their history is truly marvelous and goes hand in hand with man's work and his very slow progress in the

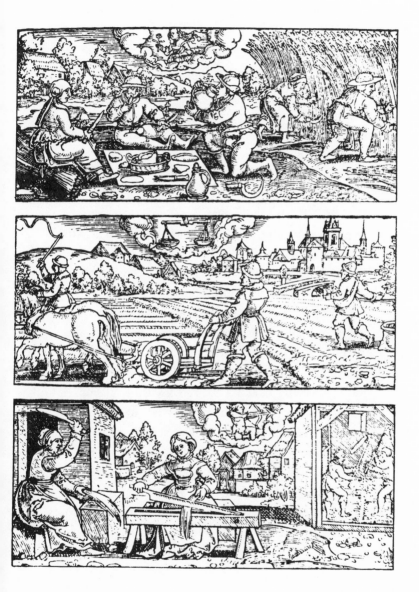

daily struggle against the outside world and against himself. Since the very beginning everything has involved technical knowledge, both man's violent exertions and his patient and monotonous efforts, shaping a stone or a piece of wood or iron to make a tool or a weapon. Here we have a very down-to-earth and essentially conservative activity, one that changes slowly and upon which a layer of science (the belated superstructure of these technical skills) is deposited slowly, if at all. Great economic concentration requires concentrated technical skills and the development of technology: take the Arsenal at Venice during the fifteenth century, Holland during the seventeenth century, or England during the eighteenth. In each case, science, though stammering and uncertain, put in its appearance. It had been brought there forcibly.

Since the earliest times, technical skills and the elements of science have mingled and spread throughout the world; there has been a constant diffusion. But diffusion was poor when it involved the assimilation of several combined technical achievements. Take navigation on the high seas and the skills that made it possible: the sternpost rudder, plus the hull constructed with lap joints, plus shipboard artillery. Or take capitalism, which also is a sum total of expedients, procedures, habits, and performances. Did deep-sea navigation, or did capitalism, make Europe supreme for the simple reason that, for each, only a number of its many components had been diffused?

But, you will ask me, "Why do your last two chapters deal with money and cities?" I cannot deny that I wanted to get these subjects out of the way before the next volume, but that obviously was not and could not be my only reason for inserting them into my first volume. The truth is that money and cities have always been a part of daily routine, yet they are present in the modern world as well. Money is a very old invention, if one subsumes under that name every means by which exchange is accelerated. And without exchange, there is no society. Cities, too, have existed since prehistoric times. They are multicenturied structures of the most ordinary way of life. But they are also multipliers, capable of adapting to change and helping to bring it about. One might say that cities and money created modernity; but conversely, according to Georges Gurvitch's law of reciprocity, modernity—the changing mass of men's lives—promoted the expansion of money and led to the growing tyranny of the cities. Cities and money are at one and the same time motors and indicators; they provoke and indicate change.

II

All this means that it is not easy to define the boundaries of the vast world of the habitual, the routine—"that great absentee in history." In reality, the habitual pervades the whole of man's life, permeating it just as the shadows of evening tint the landscape. Within this shadow, within this absence of memory and lucidity, some areas receive less light and some more light than others. It would be of prime importance if we could delineate the boundary between light and shadow, between routine and conscious decisions. If we could mark this boundary, we could distinguish between things that are to the observer's right or left or, even better, below or above him.

Imagine, therefore, the vast layer that would be formed over a given region by all the simple market-places, by the cloud of tiny dots representing markets often involving only a modest amount of merchandise. With these numerous starting points begins what we call the exchange economy, stretching between the vast world of the producer, on the one hand, and the equally enormous world of the consumer, on the other. During the centuries of the *Ancien Régime*, 1400–1800, this exchange economy was still an imperfect one. Although it had existed since time immemorial, it certainly had not succeeded in joining the total production to the total consumption, for an enormous share of the production was absorbed by the self-sufficient family or village and did not enter the market circuit.

Although the exchange form of economy was imperfect, the market economy made constant progress, connecting market towns and cities adequately enough to permit the organization of production and the direction and control of consumption. This process undoubtedly took centuries; but between these two worlds—that of production, where everything is made, and that of consumption, where everything is used up—the market economy served as the link, the driving force, the restricted but vital area from which flowed encouragement, energy, innovation, enterprise, new awarenesses, growth, and even progress. I am fond of Carl Brinkman's observation (although I do not totally agree with him) that economic history can be boiled down to the market economy, from its origins to its possible end.

So I have spent considerable time observing, describing, and bringing back to life those elementary markets within my reach. They form a frontier, a lower limit of economy. Everything outside the market has only "use value"; anything that passes through the narrow gate into the marketplace acquires "exchange value." Only if he crosses the frontier into the elementary market is the individual, or "agent,"

included in the exchange, in what I have called
economic life, in order to contrast it with material life
and also in order to distinguish it from capitalism (but
that discussion will come later).

Although a very modest consumer, the itinerant
artisan who goes from market town to market town
offering his meager services as chair-caner or chimney
sweep nevertheless belongs to the world of the
market; he expects that world to provide him with
his daily bread. If he has maintained links with his
native countryside he will go back to his village
during the harvest and vintage seasons and become a
peasant again; he will cross the market frontier once
more, but this time in the opposite direction. The
peasant himself, when he regularly sells a part of his
harvest and buys tools and clothing, is already a part
of the market. But if he comes to the market town to
sell a few items—eggs or a chicken—in order to
obtain a few coins with which to pay his taxes or buy
a plowshare, he is merely pressing his nose against the
shopwindow of the marketplace. He remains within
the vast world of self-sufficiency. The peddler who
sells small amounts in the street or throughout the
countryside is part of the world of exchanges, of
calculations, of debit and credit, no matter how
modest his exchanges and his calculations may be. The
shopkeeper is an outright agent of the market economy. He either sells items he himself has made and is

considered an artisan-shopkeeper, or he sells the products of outsiders and is regarded as a trader. A shop is always open and has the advantage of offering an uninterrupted opportunity for exchange—and for gossip—while the market is only held one or two days a week. In addition, the shop provides for exchange linked to credit, since the shopkeeper receives his merchandise on credit and sells on credit. Here a whole sequence of debits and credits is woven into the exchange.

On a level above the markets and the most basic agents involved in the exchange were the more important bourses and fairs (the former open daily and the latter held for a few days on specific dates, returning after long intervals). Even though fairs, as is generally the case, were open to small sellers and middle-sized traders, like the bourse they were dominated by large merchants (soon to be called wholesalers) who had little to do with retail sales.

In the first chapters of volume 2, which is concerned with the market economy and capitalism, I describe these various components of the market economy at length, trying to look at things in as much detail as possible. I may have taken too much pleasure in these details, and some readers may find me a bit long-winded. But is it not a good thing for history to be first of all a description, a plain observation, a scrutiny, a classification without too many previously held ideas? To see and to show is half the historian's task. To see, if possible, with his own eyes. For I can assure you that even today nothing is easier in Europe—I do not include the United States here —than to observe a municipal street market, or an old-fashioned shop, or a peddler who is quick to tell you of his travels, or a fair, or a bourse. Go to Brazil, to the back country of Bahia, or go to Kabylia or to sub-Saharan Africa, and you will find the oldest form of market still active under your very nose. In addition, if you make the effort to read them there are thousands of documents that tell of yesterday's exchanges: municipal archives, notarial registers, administrative records, and a multitude of accounts by travelers, to say nothing of painters.

Take Venice as an example. Walking through this incredibly intact city after a stroll through the archives and museums, one finds it almost possible to reconstitute scenes of the past. At Venice there were no fairs, at least no commercial ones. The *Sensa*, a fair held in mid-August for the feast of the Ascension, was a festival with sellers' stands erected in the Piazza di San Marco, with masks, music, and the spectacular ritual of the Wedding of the Doge and the Sea, near San Niccolò. A few markets were held in the Piazza di San Marco, especially the market for precious gems and equally precious furs. But the great commercial specta-cle, yesterday as well as today, occurred in the Rialto

Square, opposite the Rialto Bridge and the Fondaco dei Tedeschi, today the main post office for the city. In about 1530, Pietro Aretino, whose house was on the Grand Canal, used to enjoy watching boats loaded with fruit and mountains of melons coming in from the islands of the lagoon to this "stomach" of Venice, for the double Rialto Square, formed by the Rialto Nuovo and the Rialto Vecchio, was the "stomach" and heart of all exchanges, of all business, great and small. A few steps away from the noisy stalls of this double square the major wholesalers of the city would meet in their Loggia, built in 1455—one could almost say in their Bourse—where each morning they would discuss confidentially their businesses, maritime insurance, and shipping. They would buy, sell, and sign contracts with one another or with merchants from outside Venice. A bit farther on were the banchieri in their narrow shops, ready to settle these transactions at once by transfers of funds from one account to another. Also close at hand—they are still on the very spot today —were the Herberia ("vegetable market"), the Pescheria ("fish market"), and, a little farther along in the old Ca' Querini, the Beccarie ("butcher shops") around the butchers' church of San Matteo, which was not destroyed until the late nineteenth century.

We might feel a bit out of our element in the hubbub of the Bourse of seventeenth-century Amsterdam, but a moneychanger of our day who happened to read the astonishing book by José de la Vega, *Confusión de confusiones* (1688), would quickly feel right at home, I suspect, in the then already complicated and sophisticated game of selling and reselling shares one did not own, using the very modern procedures of selling on term or on option. A journey to London and a stop in the famous coffeehouses of Change Alley would reveal the same tricks and acrobatics.

But enough of these descriptions. Earlier, I drew a schematic picture of the levels making up the market economy: a lower one, which comprises markets, shops, and peddlers, and an upper one, which includes fairs and bourses. Now I should like to pose two questions. How can these tools—markets, shops, peddlers, fairs, bourses—used by the exchange help us to form a general explanation of the vicissitudes suffered by the European economy during the *Ancien Régime*, 1400 to 1800? And these tools, through either similarities or contrasts, explain for us the mechanisms of the non-European economy, which we have only begun to understand in recent years? It is these two questions that I would like to tackle before the end of this chapter.

III

First of all, let me review the developments in the West during the fifteenth, sixteenth, seventeenth, and eighteenth centuries.

The fifteenth century, especially after 1450, wit-nessed a general recovery of the economy, to the benefit of the cities, which, helped by rising "indus-trial" prices at a time when "agricultural" prices were stagnant or dropping, grew at a more rapid pace than the countryside. There is no doubt that at that moment artisanal shops or, even better, urban markets were the driving force. These markets imposed their wishes upon others. The recovery can therefore be observed on the "ground floor" of economic life.

During the sixteenth century—when the repaired machinery became more complicated not only because it had resumed its former speed (the thirteenth and fourteenth centuries, before the Black Death, had been periods of free acceleration) but also because the Atlantic economy had expanded—the driving force operated at the level of the international fairs: the fairs of Antwerp, Bergen op Zoom, Frankfort, Medina del Campo, and Lyons—for a moment the very center of the West—and later the so-called Besançon fairs, which eventually came to be held at Piacenza. These were extremely sophisticated gatherings limited to currency and credit transactions. For at least forty years (1579–1621) they served as a tool of the Genoese, the uncontested masters of international finance. Raymond de Roover, innately cautious and not given to generalizations, did not hesitate to characterize the sixteenth century as the apogee of the great fairs. In the final analysis, the growth during this very active century can be viewed as a sort of penthouse to the structure, a *superstructure*, and there-fore as the ballooning out of this superstructure, swollen just then by the arrival of precious metals from America and by the system of *change et rechange*,* which caused a mass of bills and loans to circulate rapidly. The Besançon fairs, that fragile masterpiece of the Genoese bankers, would collapse in the 1620s owing to a multitude of causes that occurred simultane-ously.

Freed from the spell of the Mediterranean, the active life of the seventeenth century developed in the vast reaches of the Atlantic Ocean. The seventeenth century has often been described as a period of economic retreat or stagnation; some qualifications, however, are in order. For, although the impetus of

* Instead of using a bill of exchange for a simple transfer of money from one financial exchange or fair to another, a disguised form of credit was used—disguised in order to avoid the accusation of usury. The letter was valid for a three-month period, and each renewal for another three months involved a price increase (which represented the interest). The process went on indefinitely until the credited amount had been repaid. —Trans.

the sixteenth century undeniably came to a halt in Italy and elsewhere, the fantastic rise of Amsterdam cannot be considered a part of this economic stagnation. In any event, historians all agree on one point: whatever economic activity continued was based upon a conclusive return to an exchange of goods, in other words, to an elementary form of the exchange —all of which benefited Holland, her fleet, and the Bourse at Amsterdam. At the same time, the fair was overshadowed by bourses and trade centers,* which were to the fair what the ordinary type of shop was to the urban market, that is, a continuous stream replacing intermittent encounters. This is familiar and traditional history. But we must not focus solely upon the bourse. The splendors of Amsterdam can easily blind us to more ordinary achievements. Indeed, the seventeenth century also brought about a massive expansion of shops, another triumph of the continuous. Shops multiplied all across Europe, creating tight networks of redistribution. In 1607 Lope de Vega commented that in the Madrid of the Golden Age, "*Todo se ha vuelto tiendas,*" "Everything has been transformed into shops."

---

* A *place marchande*, or trade and change center, is a city such as Amsterdam or London, which had moneychangers, currency quotations, and usually a bourse. A bill of exchange could be sent from one of these centers to another, from one fair to another, or from a fair to a center and vice versa. Lesser cities did not quote currency rates and could not send or receive bills of exchange.—Trans.

In the eighteenth century, a century of general economic acceleration, all the tools serving the exchange were put to use in a logical manner: bourses expanded their activities; London imitated and attempted to supplant Amsterdam, which at that point was beginning to specialize as a great center of international moneylending; Genoa and Geneva participated in these risky games; Paris awoke and began to tune up; money and credit flowed freely from one trade center to another. In this environment, fairs naturally lost out. Created to facilitate the traditional type of exchange by granting fiscal advantages, among other advantages, they no longer had a raison d'être during a period of easy exchanges and credit. Nonetheless, although fairs began to decline wherever the pace of life accelerated, they spread and persisted wherever the more traditional type of economy was still found. Thus, listing fairs that were active during the eighteenth century is tantamount to pointing out the marginal regions of the European economy: in France, the region of the fairs of Beaucaire; in Italy, the Bolzano region of the Alps or the Mezzogiorno; and especially the Balkans, Poland, Russia, and toward the west, beyond the Atlantic, the New World.

It goes without saying that during this period of increased consumption and exchange, the basic urban markets and shops were livelier than ever. After all, weren't shops spreading into the villages? Even peddlers became more active. Finally came the development of what English historiography calls the *private market*, which, unlike the *public market*, was free of supervision or control by haughty officials. Long before the eighteenth century, throughout all of England the private market had begun to organize direct and often prearranged purchases from producers, buying such items as wool, wheat, and cloth directly from the farmer. In other words, it established, in opposition to the traditional controlled market, very long, autonomous commercial chains that acted freely and, moreover, that evidenced no qualms about profiting from this freedom. These chains were accepted because they were efficient, making possible the massive provisioning required by the army or by large capital cities. In short, the "stomach" of London and the "stomach" of Paris were revolutionary. Eighteenth-century Europe developed everything, including the *countermarket*.

All these observations are valid for Europe. In fact, I have discussed only Europe up to this point. Not because I wanted to see everything in terms of Europe's own peculiar way of life, through an oversimplified, Europe-centered point of view, but simply because the historian's craft was developed in Europe and because historians have been interested in

their own past. During the past few decades this situation has changed; documentation on India, Japan, and Turkey has been studied systematically, and we are beginning to learn the history of these countries from sources other than the usual old travel accounts or books written by European historians. We already know enough to ask the following question: If the exchange mechanisms that I have just described for Europe existed outside Europe—and they did exist in China, India, Japan, and the Islamic world—can they be used in a comparative analysis? The purpose of such a study would be to make, if possible, a rough comparison between non-Europe and Europe itself in an attempt to see whether the broadening chasm that developed between the two worlds during the nineteenth century was already visible before the Industrial Revolution, and whether Europe really was in advance of the rest of the globe.

One initial observation: markets are found everywhere, even in the most rudimentary societies, such as sub-Saharan Africa or the Amerindian civilization. All the more reason, therefore, for more complicated and developed societies to be literally riddled with small markets. With only a little effort we can observe or reconstruct them. In the Islamic world, just as in Europe, the cities gradually stripped the villages of their markets, swallowing them up. The largest of these markets spread out from the massive city gates over terrain that was neither rural nor urban and where the city dweller on the one hand and the farmer on the other could meet on neutral ground.

Neighborhood markets managed to worm their way into the city itself, with its narrow streets and squares. There the client could find fresh bread, a limited amount of merchandise, and, contrary to the European custom, a large number of cooked dishes —meatballs, grilled sheeps' heads, fritters, and cakes. The main commercial centers—which were a combination of markets, shops, and covered markets like those found in Europe—were the fonduks or bazaars, such as the Bezestan of Istanbul.

There was one peculiarity about Indian markets: every single village had its market, owing to the necessity of using the banyan trader as an intermediary to transform payments in kind received within the village community into money to pay either the Great Mogul or the lords of his court. Should we view this swarm of village markets in India as a flaw preventing urbanism from taking hold? Or, on the contrary, should we view the banyan trader as carrying on a sort of "private market" that gained control of production at its very source, the village itself?

The most astonishing organization of the elementary market was surely that of China, where it was strictly, almost mathematically, based on geography. For a market town or small city, mark a dot on a sheet of paper. Around this point mark six to ten dots for villages, all at a distance permitting the peasant to go to the town and return in a single day. This geometric grouping—a dot in the middle with ten dots around it—is what in France we might call a canton, the sphere of influence exerted by a market town. In practice this market was divided up according to the town's streets and squares, and close at hand were usurers, public scribes, secondhand shops, the stalls of snack sellers, and tea and saki houses. G. William Skinner was right: the womb of rural China was this cantonal space, not the village itself. In view of this, it should be easy to accept that the market towns in turn were satellites of a city, which they surrounded at an appropriate distance, which they supplied with food, and which served as their link to the distant trade routes and to merchandise not produced on the spot. Indeed, that market towns and cities formed a single system is evidenced by the fact that the calendars of each were organized to avoid any conflict in schedule. Peddlers and artisans constantly moved from one market to the next and from one market town to another, for in China the artisan's shop was portable and his services were procured in the marketplace. Thus, the blacksmith or the barber would do his work at a customer's house. In short, the vast Chinese territory was crossed and enlivened by chains of regular markets, all linked to one another and all closely supervised.

Shops and peddlers also abounded in China; but fairs and bourses, the more intricate cogwheels of the mechanism, were lacking. A few fairs did exist, but they were of secondary importance and were held on the borders of Mongolia or at Canton for the benefit of foreign traders, who were in this way kept under surveillance.

Thus one of two factors must have been involved: either the Chinese government was hostile to these higher forms of exchange, or else the capillary system of the elementary market was adequate, and the Chinese economy did not need veins or arteries. For either of these two reasons, or for both of them, the exchange in China was virtually decapitated, sawed off, and I shall indicate in a subsequent chapter that this was an extremely important factor in the nonde-velopment of Chinese capitalism.

The upper levels of the exchange were more highly developed in Japan, where a network of great mer-chants was very well organized. They were also better developed in Insulinde,* an old merchant crossroads with regularly held fairs and bourses—if that term can be applied, as it is for fifteenth- and sixteenth-century Europe, to the daily meetings of important merchants at a given place. For example, in 1619 at Bantam, long the island of Java's most active city, even after the founding of Batavia, wholesale merchants met daily in one of the city squares as the market drew to a close.

India offers the best example of a country of fairs, which in its case were religious and commercial meetings combined, since they were generally held at places of pilgrimage. The entire peninsula was set in

---

*Insulinde was variously called Malaysia, the Malay Archipelago, the Indian Archipelago, the East Indies, or Indonesia. This term includes the Sunda Islands (chief among which are Java, Borneo, and Sumatra), the Moluccas or Spice Islands, New Guinea, and the Philippines, but ex-cludes the Andaman-Nicobar group.—Trans.

motion by these gigantic assemblages. Let us admire
their omnipresence and their size; but were they not
signs of a traditional economy that in some ways was
focused on the past? By contrast, fairs throughout the
Islamic world, although they existed, were not as
numerous or as large as those in India. Such exceptions
as the fairs of Mecca merely prove the rule. Indeed,
Moslem cities, overdeveloped and overdynamic,
stressed the mechanisms and instruments of the upper
exchange level. Promissory notes circulated just as
commonly as they did in India and went hand in hand
with the use of cash. A whole network of credit and
commercial organizations connected Moslem cities
with the Far East. One English traveler returning
from the Indies in 1759 and about to start overland
from Basra to Constantinople did not want to deposit
his money with the East India Company at Surat. He
deposited 2,000 piasters in cash with a banker at
Basra, who gave him a "letter in the lingua franca" to
a banker at Aleppo. In theory he should have made a
profit, but he did not gain as much as he was entitled
to. No one wins every time.

In summary, when compared with the economies of
the rest of the world, the European economy seems to
have been more developed thanks to its superior
instruments and tools: the bourse and various forms of
credit. But without exception, all the mechanisms and

expedients of the exchange can be found outside Europe. However, such mechanisms were developed and used in varying degrees, so that a hierarchy can be seen: at the top, Japan, perhaps Insulinde, and Islam; on the second level, and not very far behind, India, with the credit network developed by its banyan traders, its practice of lending money for highly speculative ventures, and its maritime insurance; and lastly, at the bottom, China, just above thousands of primitive economies.

This ranking of world economies in comparison with one another is not without significance. I shall keep this hierarchy in mind in the next chapter, when I shall attempt to evaluate the positions occupied by the market economy and by capitalism. Indeed, this vertical ranking will permit my analysis to bear fruit. Above the enormous mass of daily life, the market economy cast out its nets and kept the network alive. And it was usually above the market economy itself that capitalism prospered. One might say that the economy of the entire world is a succession of different altitudes, as in a relief map.

 The Market
Economy and
Capitalism

In the first chapter I charted a vast economic sector. Characterized by self-sufficiency from the fifteenth to the eighteenth century, this sector remained essentially outside the exchange economy. Until the eighteenth century, and beyond, even the most developed areas of Europe were riddled with pockets that scarcely participated in the general life of the subcontinent and that in their isolation continued obstinately to exist on their own, almost entirely turned inward upon themselves.

Now I would like to discuss those exchange relationships that I call both the *market economy* and *capitalism*. This double name indicates that I am making a distinction between these two sectors, which, I believe, are not the same thing. Let me repeat myself. Until the eighteenth century these two types of activity—the *market economy* and *capitalism*—affected only a minority, and the mass of mankind remained encapsulated within the vast domain of *material life*. Although the market economy was expanding and although it already covered vast areas and had at times been spectacularly successful, it still rather frequently lacked amplitude. And those phenomena of the *Ancien Régime* I wrongly or rightly call *capitalism* were the offshoots of a brilliant, sophisticated, but restricted layer, which did not grasp economic life as a whole and did not create (here the exception confirms the rule) a "mode of production" of its own that was likely to be self-seeded. Indeed, this capitalism, which is usually called *merchant capitalism*, was a long way from controlling or manipulating the market economy as a whole, although such an economy was its indispensable precondition. And yet the national, international, and world-wide role of capitalism was already clear.

I

The market economy as I have already described it confronts us with few ambiguities. Indeed, historians have placed it at the center of the stage. They all consider it to be of prime importance. In comparison, production and consumption are worlds that have scarcely been explored by quantitative research, a field only now being developed. It is not easy to understand these vast domains.

By contrast, the market economy is a constant subject of conversation. It fills page after page in urban archives, private archives of merchant families, judicial and administrative archives, debates of chambers of commerce, and notarial records. So, how can one avoid noticing it and becoming interested in it? It is continually onstage.

The danger obviously lies in seeing only the market economy, in describing it with an abundance of detail suggestive of an invasive, persistent presence, when it is really only a fragment of a vast whole. For by its very nature, the market economy is reduced to playing the role of a link between production and consumption, and until the nineteenth century it was merely a layer—more or less thick and resilient, but at times very thin—between the ocean of daily life that lay stretched out beneath it and the capitalistic mechanism that more than once manipulated it from above.

Few historians have a clear understanding of this limited function of the market economy, whose true role is marked out and defined by this very restriction. Witold Kula is among the few who have not let their vision become obscured by the highs and lows of price curves and by the crises, the distant correlations, and the unifying trends of the market—that is, by every-thing that makes the regular increase in the volume of trade tangible. To use one of Kula's metaphors, one must keep looking down into the well, into the deepest water, down into material life, which is related to market prices but is not always affected or changed by them. So, any economic history that is not written on two levels—that of the well's rim and that of the depths—runs the risk of being appallingly incomplete.

Still, it is clear that from the fifteenth to the eighteenth century the area forming the lively world of the market economy steadily increased. The harbin-ger and proof of this is the dominolike variation in market prices across the globe. For prices fluctuated throughout the entire world: in Japan and China, in India and throughout the Islamic world (for example, in the Turkish Empire), and in those parts of America where gold and silver played a role at an early date—that is, in New Spain, Brazil, and Peru. All these prices were more or less related, and changed one after the other with a varying degree of time-lag, a time-lag that is scarcely noticeable throughout Europe as a whole, where economies were closely linked to one another, but one that, by contrast, took at least twenty years to reach India, not showing up

until the late sixteenth and early seventeenth centuries.

In short, for better or for worse, some sort of
economy links the various world markets, and this
economy drags in its wake a very few luxury commod-
ities and also precious metals, those first-class travelers who were already making around-the-world tours.
The Spanish pieces of eight, struck from American
silver, crossed the Mediterranean, traveled across the
Turkish Empire and Persia, reaching India and China.
From 1572 on, after a stop at Manila, American silver
also crossed the Pacific and once again ended up in
China, by this new route.

These links, these chains, these exchanges, these
indispensable comings and goings—how could they
fail to attract historians? Such spectacles fascinate
modern historians, just as they fascinated people of
their day. But what did even the very first economists
really study, if not supply and demand in the market?
What was the economic policy of meddlesome cities,
if not the supervision, stocking, and prices of their
markets? And when the prince's decrees began to
show concern with economic policy, was it not in
order to protect the national market—and, by exten-
sion, the national flag—and to promote national
industries linked to domestic and foreign markets? It
is within this restricted and sensitive area of the

market that logical action is possible. So in the end, people believed, rightly or wrongly, that exchanges play a decisive role as a balancing force, that through competition they smooth out uneven spots and adjust supply and demand, and that the market is a hidden and benevolent god, Adam Smith's "invisible hand," the self-regulating market of the nineteenth century and the keystone of the economy, as long as one sticks to *laissez faire, laissez passer*.

In this there is an element of truth, an element of bad faith, and also some self-deception. Can we forget how many times the market was diverted or distorted and prices were arbitrarily fixed by de facto or legal monopolies? And above all, even if we accept the virtues of the competitive market ("the first computer available to men," according to Oskar Lange), we must at least point out that the market was but an imperfect link between production and consumption, if only because to some degree it remained incomplete. Let me stress the word *incomplete*. Actually, I believe in the virtues and the importance of a market economy, but I do not think of this economy as excluding all other forms. Yet, until very recently economists based their reasoning solely on the pattern and lessons of the market economy. For Turgot, "circulation" constituted the whole of economic life. Likewise, much later, David Ricardo could see only the narrow but rapid river of the market economy. And although economists, taught by experience, ceased defending the automatic virtues of laissez faire more than fifty years ago, the myth has not yet been eradicated from public opinion or from contemporary political discussions.

II

Finally, when I tossed the word *capitalism* into the ring and applied it to a century during which its very existence is not always accepted, I did so because I needed a term other than *market economy* to designate two quite distinct activities. I certainly did not intend to let the wolf into the sheepfold. I am well aware (historians have repeated it so many times, and rightly so) that the controversial term *capitalism* is ambiguous and loaded with contemporary and, possibly, anachronistic connotations. If I threw caution to the winds and let the word in, it was for a number of reasons.

First of all, certain mechanisms occurring between the fifteenth and eighteenth centuries are crying out for a name all their own. When we look at them closely, we see that fitting them into a slot in the ordinary market economy would be almost absurd. One word does come spontaneously to mind: *capitalism*. Irritated, one shoos it out the door, and almost immediately it climbs in through the window. There is no adequate substitute for this word, and that fact alone is symptomatic. As Andrew Shonfield, the American economist, says, the best reason for using the word *capitalism*, no matter how much people run it down, is that no one has found a better word. It undoubtedly has the disadvantage of dragging count-less controversies and discussions along after one. But these controversies—whatever their merit—cannot be avoided; we cannot carry on discussions and behave as if they did not exist. An even greater disadvantage is that the word is loaded with meanings acquired in our day. For *capitalism* in its broadest sense dates from the beginning of the twentieth century. I could somewhat arbitrarily state that it was launched in 1902 when Werner Sombart published his well-known *Der moderne Kapitalismus*. Marx was virtually unaware of the word. I am, therefore, directly threatened with the worst of sins, the sin of anachro-nism. No capitalism before the Industrial Revolution, a still-young historian shouted one day: "Capital, yes, capitalism, no!"

And yet, there has never been a total break, an absolute discontinuity—or, if you prefer, a noncon-tamination—between the past, even the very distant past, and the present. Past experiences continue into the present, adding to it. Thus, many historians—and some of the best—are now discovering that the Industrial Revolution was already putting in its

appearance long before the eighteenth century. Perhaps the best evidence of this is provided by certain
underdeveloped countries that are today attempting
their own Industrial Revolution and that are failing,
even though they have a successful model right before
their eyes. In short, this dialectic that is constantly
being questioned—past, present; present, past—may
well be no less than the heart, the very raison d'être of
history itself.

III

The word *capitalism* can only be kept under control,
defined, and used in historical exploration by situat-
ing it carefully between the two underlying words
that give it its meaning: *capital* and *capitalist*. *Capital* is a
tangible reality, a congeries of easily identifiable
financial resources, constantly at work; a *capitalist* is a
man who presides or attempts to preside over the
insertion of capital into the ceaseless process of
production to which every society is destined; and
capitalism is, roughly (but only roughly) speaking, the
manner in which this constant activity of insertion is
carried on, generally for not very altruistic reasons.

The key word is *capital*. In the works of economists
it has been given the more specific meaning of *capital
goods*; it denotes not only accumulations of money but
also the usable and used results of all previously

47

accomplished work. A house is capital; stored wheat is capital; a ship or a road is capital. But capital goods only deserve that name if they are a part of the renewed process of production; the money in an unused treasure is no longer capital, nor is an unworked forest. This being so, can we name a single society that does not accumulate things, does not accumulate capital goods, does not regularly employ them in its work, and does not rebuild them through work and make them bear fruit? The smallest village in the fifteenth-century West had paths, fields cleared of

stones, cultivated lands, systematically managed forests, hedgerows, orchards, mill wheels, and grana-ries. Calculations made for the economics of the *Ancien Régime* show a ratio of one to three or four between the gross national product for one year and total capital goods (what the French call *patrimoine*, "patrimony"). This is virtually the same rate that Keynes allowed for the economies of twentieth-century societies. Each society, therefore, was backed up by reserve supplies equaling three or four years' worth of accumulated work, and it used these reserves to carry out its production successfully; for the patrimony, of course, was only partly—never totally—used for this pur-pose.

But let us move on from these problems, which you are as familiar with as I am. In fact, I owe my readers only one explanation: how I can validly distinguish *capitalism* from *market economy*. And vice versa. Please do not expect me to draw such a clear-cut distinction as: water below, and oil floating on its surface. The actual economic situation is never built upon simple foundations. But it should not be too difficult to accept my statement that there are at least two possible forms (A and B) of the so-called market economy, forms that can be discerned with a bit of care, if only through the human, economic, and social relationships they generate.

In the A category I would readily place daily market exchanges and such examples of local or relatively local trade as wheat and wood being sent to a nearby city. I would even include trade on a broader scale, as long as it is regular, predictable, routine, and open to both small and large merchants; for example, the shipping of Baltic grain from Danzig to Amsterdam during the seventeenth century, or the oil and wine trade between southern and northern Europe (in this instance I am thinking of the convoys of carts from Germany that each year went to fetch white wine in Istria).

The market held in a small town provides a good example of these "transparent" exchanges, which involve no surprises, in which each party knows in advance the rules and the outcome, and for which the always moderate profits can be roughly calculated beforehand. Such a market chiefly involves producers —peasant men and women and artisans—and clients, some from the market town itself and others from neighboring villages. From time to time three people at the very most are involved; that is, an intermediary, a third man, appears between the client and producer. This dealer can, when the occasion arises, upset or dominate the market and influence prices by stockpiling goods; even a small retailer can flout the law and deal with peasants as they enter the town, purchasing their goods at a lower price, then selling them in the

market. This simple form of lawbreaking—forestal-
ling—is found on the outskirts of every market town
and to an even greater extent around the cities, and if
the parties involved have an understanding, they can
cause prices to rise.

So, even in the model market town I am picturing,
where trade was regulated, law-abiding, transparent
—"eye to eye and hand to hand," say the Germans
—exchanges typical of category B, which avoided
transparency and control, would not be totally
absent. Likewise, the regular trade resulting in the
great wheat shipments from the Baltic was transparent trade: the price curves at the point of departure,
Danzig, and at the point of arrival, Amsterdam, were
synchronous, and the profits were both certain and
moderate. But, let a famine break out in the Mediterranean—a famine such as that in the 1590s—and
international merchants representing major clients
would divert entire ships from their usual routes and
see that their cargoes were carried to Livorno or
Genoa to be sold at three or four times the normal
price. Here also economy A might bow before
economy B.

Once we begin to move up the hierarchy of
exchanges, however, the second or B type of economy
becomes predominant and forms before our very eyes a
"sphere of circulation" that is clearly different from
that formed by category A. English historians have

shown that as of the fifteenth century the traditional public market was accompanied by what they have called the private market (I would prefer to stress differences and call it the *countermarket*). For indeed, did it not try to free itself from the rules imposed upon the traditional market, rules that were often paralyzing in their excessiveness? Itinerant dealers who collected and assembled merchandise went to the homes of the producers. From the peasant they bought wool, hemp, livestock, hides, barley or wheat, and poultry. Or they might even buy these items in advance, as unshorn wool and uncut wheat. A simple note signed in the village inn or at the farm itself sealed the bargain. Then they shipped their purchases by cart, pack horse, or boat to the major cities or coastal ports. Examples of this sort of activity were to be found throughout the world, around Paris and London, at Segovia (for wool), around Naples (for wheat), in Apulia (for oil), and in Insulinde (for pepper). When he did not go to the farm itself, the itinerant dealer arranged meetings on the outskirts of the market, along the outer limits of the square where the market was held, or, more often, he conducted his business at an inn, for inns served as post stops and transport offices.

This type of exchange replaced the normal collec-tive market and substituted for it individual transac-tions based on arbitrary financial arrangements that varied according to the respective situation of the individuals involved. This fact is clearly established by the frequent lawsuits in England over the interpretation of notes signed by sellers. It is obvious that here we are dealing with unequal exchanges in which competition—the basic law of the so-called market economy—had little place and in which the dealer had two trump cards: he had broken off relations between the producer and the person who eventually received the merchandise (only the dealer knew the market conditions at both ends of the chain and hence the profit to be expected); and he had ready cash, which served as his chief ally. Thus, long chains of merchants took position between production and consumption, and it is surely their effectiveness that caused them to win acceptance, especially in supplying large cities, and that prompted the authorities to close their eyes or at least to relax controls.

Now, the longer these chains become, the more successful they are at freeing themselves from the usual regulations and controls and the more clearly the capitalistic process emerges. It becomes strikingly evident in long-distance trade, in the *Fernhandel*, which German historians have not been alone in considering the superlative commercial activity. The *Fernhandel* was a zone of free operation, *par excellence*, working over distances that protected it from the usual supervision or that permitted it to manipulate

such supervision; it might stretch from the Coroman-
del Coast or the shores of Bengal to Amsterdam and
from Amsterdam to retailers in Persia, China, or
Japan. Within this vast zone of operations the *Fern-
händler* was able to choose, and he chose whatever
would maximize his profits: Had trade with the
Antilles stopped making more than modest profits?
Never mind, in the meantime the *country trade** or the
trade with China had become twice as profitable.
One merely had to order the ships' captains to set sail
in the opposite direction.

Such huge profits resulted in sizable accumulations
of capital, especially since long-distance trade was
carried on by a mere handful of individuals. Not just
anyone could join the group. By contrast, local
commerce was divided up among a multitude of
participants. For example, in the sixteenth century
the total presumed monetary value of Portuguese
domestic trade, taken as a whole, was far superior to
that of the pepper, spice, and drug trades. But this
domestic trade often took the form of barter, of *use
value*. The spice trade formed a part of the main line of
the monetary economy. And only large merchants
conducted such trade and concentrated within their

* *"Le commerce d'Inde en Inde"* is the eighteenth-century French equivalent
of the English term *country trade,* that is, local trade in the Far East, for
example, between the Malabar Coast and Bengal or between India and
China.—Trans.

hands the abnormally large profits derived from it. The same is true for England in the early eighteenth century, the time of Daniel Defoe.

It is no accident that throughout the world a group of large merchants stands out clearly from the mass of ordinary dealers and that this group is, on the one hand, very small and, on the other, always connected with long-distance trade, among its other activities. The phenomenon can be seen by the fourteenth century in Germany, by the thirteenth century in Paris, and by the twelfth century and probably even earlier in Italian cities. Even before the emergence in the West of the first merchants, in the Islamic world the *tayir* was an importer-exporter who directed agents and factors from his home (here we already have business in a fixed place). He had nothing in common with the *hawanti*, or shopkeeper, in the sukh. In the Indian city of Agra, which in about 1640 was still enormous, a traveler noted that the title *Sogador* was given to "the one who at home in Spain would be called a *mercader*, but some of them boast the special title *Katari*, the most eminent title among those who profess, in this country, the mercantile art, and which means 'most rich merchant who is possessed of great credit.' " In the West the vocabulary used reveals similar distinctions. The *négociant* or wholesale merchant was France's *Katari*; the word *négociant* appeared during the seventeenth century. In

Italy there was a vast difference between the *mercante a taglio* and the *negoziante*; in England between the *tradesman*, or dealer, and the *merchant* based in English ports who was chiefly concerned with exporting and long-distance trade; and in Germany between the *Krämer* on the one hand and the *Kaufman* or *Kaufherr* on the other.

Need I comment that these capitalists, both in Islam and in Christendom, were friends of the prince and helpers or exploiters of the state? At an early date, from the very beginning, they went beyond "national" boundaries and were in touch with merchants in foreign commercial centers. These men knew a thousand ways of rigging the odds in their favor: the manipulation of credit and the profitable game of good money for bad, with the "good" silver or gold coins being used for major transactions to build up Capital and the "bad" copper pieces being used for the lowest salaries and for daily wages, in other words, for Labor. They possessed superior knowledge, intelligence, and culture. And around about them they grabbed up everything worth taking —land, real estate, and land rents. Who could doubt that these capitalists had monopolies at their disposal or that they simply had the power needed to eliminate competition nine times out of ten? When writing to one of his confederates at Bordeaux, a Dutch merchant advised that their plans be kept secret; otherwise, he added, "this affair will turn out like so many others in which, once competition comes into play, there is no chance to make a profit." Finally, the sheer size of their capital enabled capitalists to preserve their privileged position and to reserve for themselves the big international transactions of the day. On the one hand, this was possible because, during that period of extremely slow transportation, wide-scale trade involved long delays in the turnover of capital; it took months and sometimes years for the money invested to return swollen with its profits. On the other hand, the big merchant generally did not restrict himself solely to his capital; he had recourse to credit, to other people's money. And, in addition, capital and credit are able to move about. The papers of Francesco di Marco Datini, a merchant of Prato, near Florence, reveal that by the end of the fourteenth century letters of change were moving to and fro between Italian cities and the most active centers of European capitalism: Barcelona, Montpellier, Avignon, Paris, London, and Bruges. But such manipulations were as foreign to ordinary mortals as the supersecret deliberations of the Banque des Règlements Internationaux of Basel are to the man on the street today.

Thus, the commercial or exchange world was a world of hierarchies, starting with the humblest jobs—porters, stevedores, peddlers, carters, and sailors—and moving up to cashiers, shopkeepers, brokers of various sorts, and moneylenders, and finally reaching the merchants. At first glance we are surprised that, as the progress brought by the market economy affected commercial society as a whole, specialization and the division of labor increased, except at the summit, the level of the merchant-capitalists. And so this process of breaking down functions into several smaller ones, this process of modernization, was at first evident only at the base of the pyramid: shops and peddlers began to specialize. Specialization did not occur at the top of the pyramid, for until the nineteenth century the top-level merchant virtually never restricted himself to a single activity. He was, of course, a merchant, but he never handled one product exclusively, and as circumstances directed he could as well become a ship chandler, an underwriter, a lender, a borrower, a financier, a banker, or even a "manufacturer" or an agricultural manager. In eighteenth-century Barcelona the retail shopkeeper or *botiguer* always had a specialization; he would sell either linens or woolen cloths or spices, and so forth. If one day he happened to accumulate enough wealth to become a wholesaler, he would at once move from specialization to nonspecialization. From then on any lucrative transaction within his reach would constitute his "specialization." This anomaly has often been commented upon, but the usual explanation is scarcely sufficient. The merchant, we are told, divided his activities among various sectors in order to limit his risks; if he lost on cochineal, he might gain on spices. If he botched a business deal, he might come out ahead by taking advantage of exchange rates or by lending money to a peasant to create an annuity. In short, he would follow the advice of the proverb that counseled him not to put all his eggs into one basket.

I believe, first, that the merchant did not specialize because no one branch of the commerce available to him was sufficiently developed to absorb all his energy. It has too often been accepted that the capitalism of the past was small because it lacked capital; that it took a long time to accumulate sufficient capital for capital-ism to blossom. In fact, the correspondence of mer-chants and the memoranda of chambers of commerce reveal capital sums looking vainly to be invested. Lacking other and more profitable places for invest-ment, the capitalist would be tempted to acquire land, a safe investment and one that conferred social distinction, but sometimes he would also buy land that could be farmed in a modern manner and become a source of substantial income, as was the case in England, the Venetian state, and elsewhere. Or the merchant would allow himself to be tempted by urban real estate speculation. Or by prudent but repeated incursions into the industrial sector, for example, the mining business during the fifteenth and sixteenth centuries. But it is significant that, with a few possible exceptions, he showed no interest in the system of production and was content, through the *putting-out system*, to control artisanal production in order better to see to the commercialization of this production. Compared with the artisan and the putting-out system, manufactures until the nineteenth century represented only a very small share of total production.

Second, I believe that if the large merchant changed his activities so frequently, it was because high profits were constantly shifting from one sector to another. Capitalism is essentially conjunctural, that is, it flourishes according to the dictates of changes in the economic situation. Even today one of capitalism's greatest strengths remains its ability to adapt and to change.

Third, I think that one specialization sometimes did tend to develop in commercial life: money trading. But its success never lasted long, as if the economic edifice could not pump enough nourishment up to this high point of the economy. After its brief moment of glory, the Florentine bank collapsed, along with the Bardi and Peruzzi families during the fourteenth century and again with the Medicis during the fifteenth. After 1579 the Genoese fairs of Piacenza became a clearing system for almost all European payments, but the extraordinary adventure of these Genoese bankers lasted less than fifty years, until 1621. Amsterdam brilliantly dominated the European credit network in its turn during the seventeenth century; this experiment also ended in failure during the following century. Financial capitalism only succeeded in the nineteenth century, after the period 1830–60, when the banks grabbed up everything, both industry and merchandise, and when the economy in general was strong enough to support this edifice permanently.

Let me summarize. There are two types of exchange: one is down-to-earth, is based on competition, and is almost transparent; the other, a higher form, is sophisticated and domineering. Neither the same mechanisms nor the same agents govern these two types of activity, and the capitalist sphere is located in the higher form. I am not denying the possible existence of a clever and ruthless village capitalist in wooden shoes. According to what Professor Viktor Dalin of Moscow told me, Lenin stated that even within the socialist world, the village market, having once regained its freedom, might well reconstitute the whole tree of capitalism. I am also not denying that a microcapitalism existed among shopkeepers; Alexander Gerschenkron thinks that true capitalism was born there. The basic inequality of partners that underlies the capitalistic process is visible on every level of social life. But in the end, it was at the very summit of society that capitalism unfolded first, asserted its strength, and revealed itself. It is on the level of the Bardis, the Jacques Coeurs, the Jakob Fuggers, the John Laws, or the Neckers that we must conduct our search, that we have a chance of discovering capitalism.

If no distinction is usually made between capitalism and the market economy, it is because they both moved ahead at the same rate, from the Middle Ages to the present, and because capitalism has often been presented as the motivating force or the flowering of economic progress. In reality, everything rested upon the very broad back of material life; when material life expanded, everything moved ahead, and the market economy also expanded rapidly and reached out at the expense of material life. Now, capitalism always benefits from such expansion. I do not believe that Joseph Schumpeter was right in considering the entrepreneur a sort of *deus ex machina*. I persist in my belief that the determining factor was the movement as a whole and that the extensiveness of any capitalism is in direct proportion to the underlying economy.

IV

The preserve of the few, capitalism is unthinkable without society's active complicity. It is of necessity a reality of the social order, a reality of the political order, and even a reality of civilization. For in a certain manner, society as a whole must more or less consciously accept capitalism's values. But this does not always happen.

Any highly developed society can be broken down into several "ensembles": the economy, politics, culture, and the social hierarchy. The economy can only be understood in terms of the other "ensembles," for it both spreads itself about and opens its own doors to its neighbors. There is action and interaction. That rather special and partial form of the economy that is capitalism can only be fully explained in the light of these contiguous "ensembles" and their encroachments; only then will it reveal its true face.

Thus, the modern state, which did not create capitalism but only inherited it, sometimes acts in its favor and at other times acts against it; it sometimes allows capitalism to expand and at other times destroys its mainspring. Capitalism only triumphs when it becomes identified with the state, when it is the state. In its first great phase, that of the Italian city-states of Venice, Genoa, and Florence, power lay in the hands of the moneyed elite. In seventeenth-century Holland the aristocracy of the Regents governed for the benefit and even according to the directives of the businessmen, merchants, and money-lenders. Likewise, in England the Glorious Revolution of 1688 marked the accession of business similar to that in Holland. France was more than a century behind; only with the July Revolution of 1830 did the commercial bourgeoisie become comfortably ensconced in the government.

So the state was either favorable or hostile to the financial world according to its own equilibrium and its own ability to stand firm. The same was true for culture and religion. In theory, religion, a conservative force, said no to innovations involving the market, money, speculation, and usury. But the Church came to an agreement with the financial world. It continued to say no, but eventually it said yes to the overwhelming exigencies of the century. In a nutshell, it accepted an *aggiornamento*, to use the expression coined after Vatican II, or what used to be called a "modernism." (Augustin Renaudet used to tell how Saint Thomas Aquinas [1225?–74] formulated the first modernism destined one day to succeed.) But although religion, and therefore culture, removed such obstacles at a relatively early date, the Church continued to oppose matters on principle, especially in the case of interest-bearing loans, which it condemned as usury. It has even been said, a bit hastily it is true, that these scruples were only removed by the Reformation and that this is the true explanation of capitalism's development in the countries of northern Europe. For Max Weber, capitalism

in the modern sense of the word was no more and no less than a creation of Protestantism or, to be even more accurate, of Puritanism.

All historians have opposed this tenuous theory, although they have not managed to be rid of it once and for all. Yet it is clearly false. The northern countries took over the place that earlier had so long and so brilliantly been occupied by the old capitalist centers of the Mediterranean. They invented nothing, either in technology or in business management. Amsterdam copied Venice, as London would subsequently copy Amsterdam, and as New York would one day copy London. What was involved on each occasion was a shift of the center of gravity of the world economy, for economic reasons that had nothing whatever to do with the basic or secret nature of capitalism. The definitive shift at the end of the sixteenth century from the Mediterranean to the North Sea represented the victory of a new region over an old one. It also represented a vast change of scale. Aided by the new rise of the Atlantic, the general economy, trade, and even the monetary supply expanded. And once again the rapid growth of the market economy—which faithfully kept its appointment at Amsterdam—supported on its broad back the expanded constructions of capitalism. All things considered, I believe Max Weber's error stems essentially from his exaggeration of capitalism's role as promoter of the modern world.

But the basic problem does not lie there. Indeed, the real fate of capitalism was determined by its encounter with social hierarchies.

Every evolved society incorporates several hierarchies, let us call them staircases permitting exit from the ground floor where the mass of the population —Werner Sombart's *Grundvolk*—vegetates: a religious hierarchy, a political hierarchy, a military hierarchy, and various financial hierarchies. Depending upon the century and the locality, oppositions, compromises, and alliances develop among them, and sometimes they even seem to merge. In thirteenth-century Rome the political and religious hierarchies merged, but around the city the land and livestock were creating a dangerous class of great nobles, while the Sienese bankers to the Curia were already climbing very high. In late-fourteenth-century Florence, the old feudal nobility and the new merchant upper bourgeoisie had become one, forming a moneyed elite that in a logical fashion set about gaining political control. In other social contexts, however, a political hierarchy might crush all other hierarchies; such was the case in the China of the Mings and the Manchus. Such was also the case—although in a less outright and less consistent manner—for the monarchical France of the *Ancien Régime*, which long forced merchants, even rich ones, to play a role lacking in prestige while pushing to the forefront the decisive hierarchy of the nobility. In France under Louis XIII the way to power lay in drawing near the king and the court. The first real step up in the career of Richelieu, holder of the shabby bishopric of Luçon, was to become almoner to Queen Mother Marie de Médicis, and hence be admitted to court and enter the restricted circle of those governing.

Each society has its own channels through which individual ambition can be achieved. Each society has its *type* of success. In the West, although individual successes were not rare, history repeatedly taught the same lesson: such successes must almost always be credited to the assets amassed by vigilant, attentive families striving to increase their fortune and their influence bit by bit. Their ambition went hand in hand with patience; it was a long-term sort of ambition. Must we therefore sing the praises and merits of long-lived families, that is, of lineages? To do so would mean, in the case of the West, to confer stardom upon what is loosely called—employing a term that came into use quite late—the history of the bourgeoisie, bearer of the capitalistic process, creator or user of a solid hierarchy that would form the backbone of capitalism. For in order to lay firm foundations for its fortune and its power, capitalism successively or simultaneously depended upon local trade, upon usury, upon long-distance trade, upon the venal administrative office, upon the land—a sure investment and one that, in addition, conferred obvious prestige, indeed, more prestige than we might think—and upon society itself. If one looks closely at these long family chains and at the slow accumulation of estates and preferments, the shift in Europe from the feudal regime to the capitalist one becomes almost understandable. The feudal regime benefited seigneurial families, for it was a durable *form* that distributed that basic treasure, the land. In other words, it created an essentially stable social regime. Over the centuries the "bourgeoisie" was a parasite clinging to this privileged class, living from it, cheek to cheek, and profiting from its errors, its love of luxury, its idleness, and its improvidence in order to seize its possessions—often thanks to usury—and finally to slip into the ranks of the nobility. But other bourgeois were there to renew the attack and begin the old struggle anew. In a word, this was a long-term parasitism: the bourgeoisie ceaselessly destroyed the ruling class in order to satisfy its own appetite. But its rise was slow and patient and its ambition was constantly being passed on to children and grandchildren. And over and over again.

This type of society, derived from a feudal society and still half feudal itself, is one in which property and social privileges are relatively protected, in which families can enjoy relative tranquillity, since ownership is or wants to be considered sacrosanct, and in which each individual remains more or less in his place. Now, calm or relatively calm social waters are needed if *accumulation* is to take place, if lineages are to grow and be maintained, if the monetary economy is to help capitalism emerge at last. In the process, capitalism destroys certain bastions of upper society, but it does so in order to reconstruct to its own advantage other bastions that are equally solid and durable.

These long gestation periods for family fortunes, ending one day in spectacular success, are so familiar to us, both in the past and in the present, that it is difficult for us to realize that this is a basic character- istic of Western societies. We only truly notice it when we leave the West and observe the different spectacle provided by non-European societies. In those societies, what I call—or would like to call —capitalism generally encounters social obstacles that are difficult or impossible to hurdle. Ironically, these very obstacles provide the clues to a general explanation.

Japanese society is in this respect atypical, for there the process was roughly the same as in Europe: a feudal society deteriorated slowly and capitalism finally burst forth (Japan being the country where merchant dynasties lasted the longest, since some of them, dating from the seventeenth century, are still prospering today). But comparative studies of the history of societies can offer only these two exam- ples—the West and Japan—of societies that have moved virtually on their own momentum from the feudal to the monetary order. Elsewhere the respec- tive positions of the state, of privilege owing to rank, and of privilege owing to wealth were very different, and from these differences I shall try to draw a lesson.

Consider China or Islam. In China the incomplete statistics available to us give the impression that vertical social mobility was greater there than in Europe. It is not that the number of privileged persons was relatively greater, but that Chinese society was much less stable than European society. The open door, the open hierarchy, took the form of examinations for the rank of mandarin. Although such examinations were not always conducted with absolute honesty, they were theoretically accessible to all social groups, infinitely more accessible in any event than the great universities of the West during the nineteenth century. The examinations that provided access to the high rank of mandarin actually amounted to a new shuffling of the cards used in the social game, literally a constant "new deal." However, those who reached the summit only did so in a precarious fashion, receiving a sort of lifetime title. And the fortunes they often accumulated on such occasions did little to lay the foundations of what in Europe would be called the *grandes familles*, the "great families." In addition, very rich and very powerful families were on principle suspect to the state, which alone had the right to own land and levy taxes on the peasants and which closely supervised mining, industrial, and commercial enterprises. Despite the local complicity of merchants and corrupt mandarins, the Chinese state showed constant hostility to the spread of capitalism. Each time capitalism expanded as a result of favorable circumstances, it would eventually be brought back under control by a state that was virtually totalitarian (with all the pejorative present-day meanings of this word removed). True Chinese capitalism only existed outside China—for example, in Insulinde, where the Chinese merchant carried on his business and established his domain in complete freedom.

In the vast world of Islam, especially prior to the eighteenth century, land ownership was temporary, for there, as in China, land legally belonged to the prince. Using the terminology of the European *Ancien Régime*, historians might call such holdings *bénéfices* (that is, possessions given for one's lifetime), as contrasted with family *fiefs*. In other words, seigneuries—that is, lands, villages, and land rents—were distributed by the state (in a manner reminiscent of the way the old Carolingian state had proceeded) and became available once more whenever the beneficiary died. For the prince this provided a way of paying foot soldiers and horsemen and of being assured of their future loyalty. When the lord died, his seigneury and all his possessions reverted to the Sultan of Istanbul or the Great Mogul of Delhi. It must be pointed out that, as long as their authority lasted, these great princes could change the composition of the ruling society, the elite class, as they might change their shirts, and they did not hesitate to do so. Thus, the summit of society was frequently renewed, and families were unable to become firmly entrenched. André Raymond's recent study of eighteenth-century Cairo shows us that the great merchants there rarely were able to maintain their positions for more than a generation. They were devoured by political society. If the life of the Indian merchant was less uncertain, it was because it developed within the protection of the merchant and banking castes, rather than in the unstable society at the top of the pyramid.

By now the rather simple, plausible theory I have proposed should be easier to understand: the growth and success of capitalism require certain social conditions. They require a certain tranquillity in the social order and a certain neutrality, or weakness, or permissiveness by the state. In the West, this permissiveness appeared in varying degrees; it was chiefly owing to social reasons, reasons deeply rooted in the past, that the French nation has always been less favorable to capitalism than, say, England has been.

I believe there will be no serious objections on this score. But now a new problem becomes apparent. Capitalism needs a hierarchy. But what is a hierarchy per se to a historian who can conjure up a procession of hundreds and hundreds of societies, all of which have hierarchies, all of which have at their summits a handful of privileged individuals who hold the power? Hierarchies existed in the past, in thirteenth-century Venice, in Europe during the *Ancien Régime*, in the France of Thiers, or in the France of 1936 when popular slogans denounced the "200 families" in power. But they also existed in Japan, in China, in

74

Turkey, and in India. And they still exist today, even in the United States. Capitalism does not invent hierarchies, any more than it invented the market, or production, or consumption; it merely uses them. In the long procession of history, capitalism is the late-comer. It arrives when everything is ready.

In other words, the specific problem of the hierarchy goes beyond capitalism, transcends it, controls it a priori. Alas, noncapitalist societies have not suppressed hierarchies. All of which opens the door to the long deliberations I included in my book, without coming to any conclusions, however. For this is indubitably the key problem, the problem of problems. Must the hierarchy, the dependence of one man upon another, be destroyed? "Yes," said Jean-Paul Sartre in 1968. But is such a thing really possible?

Capitalism and Dividing Up the World

In the first two chapters I spread all the pieces of the puzzle before you, sometimes separately, sometimes grouped together in an arbitrary fashion, whichever seemed most convenient for the explanation I was making. I shall work the puzzle in this chapter, whose very title reveals my goal: to establish the connection between capitalism, its development and modes of action, and a general history of the world.

A *history*: a chronological sequence of forms and experiences. The *whole world*: the unity that between the fifteenth and eighteenth centuries took shape and progressively made its weight felt in every aspect of human life and in every society, economy, and civilization of the globe.

This world manifests itself in an atmosphere of inequality. The present-day image—wealthy nations versus underdeveloped ones—was already the case, *mutatis mutandis*, from the fifteenth to the eighteenth century. Of course, from the days of Jacques Coeur, to Jean Bodin, to Adam Smith, and on to Keynes, the rich and the poor countries were not constantly the same ones; the wheel did turn. But the law governing the world has scarcely changed; the globe continues structurally to be divided among the haves and the have-nots. A sort of world society exists, a much enlarged but still recognizable version of ordinary hierarchized society. Microcosm and macrocosm, but both cut from the same cloth. Why? I shall try to answer this, but I may not succeed. The historian has less trouble seeing the hows than the whys and can more clearly discern the consequences than the origins of major problems. All the more reason, of course, for him to become excited about discovering these origins, which so routinely elude him, thumbing their noses all the while.

I

Once again a working vocabulary must be established. Indeed, two terms must be employed: *economy*

of the world and *world economy*, the latter the more important of the two. By *economy of the world* I mean the
world economy as a whole, the "market of the
universe," as Sismondi called it. By *world-economy*—a
word I forged on the pattern of the German word
Weltwirtschaft—I mean the economy of only one
portion of our planet, to the degree that it forms an
economic *whole*. Long ago I wrote that the Mediterranean of the sixteenth century was in itself a *Weltwirtschaft*, a world-economy, or, to use another German
expression, *"eine Welt für sich,"* a world unto itself.

A world-economy can be described as having three
facets:

1. It occupies a given geographic space; thus it has
limits that mark it off and that vary, albeit somewhat
slowly. Breaks inevitably occur from time to time, but
at long intervals; for example, following the Age of
Discovery of the late fifteenth century, or in 1689,
when Peter the Great opened Russia to the European
economy. Imagine the sort of break that would occur
in the West as we know it today were a free, total,
and definitive opening of the Soviet and Chinese
economies to occur.

2. A world-economy always has a pole or a
center, represented by one dominant city, in the past a
city-state, today a capital city—that is, an economic
capital, New York rather than Washington, D.C. In
addition, two centers can exist simultaneously and for

a prolonged period within a single world-economy, as did Rome and Alexandria under Caesar Augustus, Anthony, and Cleopatra; Venice and Genoa before the war of Chioggia (1378–81); or London and Amsterdam during the eighteenth century, before the definitive exclusion of Holland. For one of these two centers is always eliminated in the end. Thus, in 1929, after some hesitation, the center of the world unquestionably shifted from London to New York.

3. Every world-economy is divided into successive zones. There is the heart, that is, the region about the center—the United Provinces (but not all the United Provinces) when Amsterdam dominated the world during the seventeenth century; or England (but not all of England) when London definitively supplanted Amsterdam after the 1780s. Then come intermediate zones about this central pivot. Finally, there are the very wide peripheral areas, which, in the division of labor characteristic of the economy-world, are subordinates rather than true participants. Within these peripheral zones, life often resembles purgatory or even hell. Their mere geographical location provides sufficient explanation for this.

These hasty observations should be backed up by comments and proofs; these will be available in volume 3 of *Civilisation matérielle et capitalisme*. A fine description of the problem is to be found in Immanuel Wallerstein's recent book, *The Modern World-System*.

It is unimportant that I disagree with the author on certain points and on one or two general positions. Our points of view are basically identical, even though Wallerstein believes that the only world-economy was the European one, which was not founded until the sixteenth century, whereas I believe that by the Middle Ages and even in antiquity, long before Europeans knew the world in its totality, the globe was already divided up into more or less centralized and more or less coherent economic zones, that is, into several world-economies that coexisted.

These coexisting economies, which carried on only an extremely limited number of exchanges among themselves, divided up the populated areas of the planet, creating rather vast frontier regions, which, with few exceptions, commerce generally saw little advantage in crossing. Until Peter the Great, Russia (Muscovy, to be exact) was one of these self-contained world-economies, living essentially by and upon itself. The immense Turkish Empire was also a world-economy, until the end of the eighteenth century. On the other hand, the Empire of Charles V or Philip II was not, despite its immensity; from the outset it was part of an old and active European-based economic network. For, well before Christopher Columbus's voyage in 1492, Europe and the Mediterranean, with its antennae directed toward the Far East, formed a world-economy, at that point revolving about the glories of Venice. This world-economy expanded during the Age of Discovery, annexing the Atlantic, its islands and coastlines, and finally the inner reaches of the American continent, which were only laid hold of after a long while. It also multiplied its links with other still-autonomous world-economies: India, Insulinde, and China. Meanwhile, its center of gravity within Europe shifted from the south to the north, first to Antwerp and then to Amsterdam, and not—let me point out—to Seville or Lisbon, the centers of the Spanish and Portuguese empires.

Thus it is possible to lay a piece of tracing paper over the historical map of the world and draw a rough outline of the world-economies to be found during any given period. Since these economies changed slowly, we have all the time in the world to study them, to watch them in action, and to weigh their influence. Slow to change contours, they reveal the presence of an underlying history of the world. I can merely evoke this deep-down history, for my sole aim here is to show how the successive, European-based world-economies explain or fail to explain the capitalist process and its expansion. I would not hesitate to state at the outset that these typical world-economies were the wombs that gave birth to European and, later, world capitalism. At any rate, that is the explanation toward which I am cautiously and slowly moving.

II

A deep-down history. I have not discovered this history; I should simply like to reveal its importance, and, as Lucien Febvre would have said, "confer dignity upon it." That is already a great deal. I hope to convince you of this as I dwell at some length upon the changes that occurred in the center—the *decenterings*—of the world-economies, and then upon the subdividing of every world-economy into concentric zones.

Each time a decentering occurs, a recentering takes place, as if the world-economy cannot live without a center of gravity, without a pole. And since these decenterings and recenterings occur infrequently, they are all the more important. In the case of Europe and the zones it annexed, a centering occurred in the 1380s and gave Venice the advantage. In about 1500 there was an abrupt and gigantic shift from Venice to Antwerp; then the period 1550–60 brought a return to the Mediterranean, but this time in favor of Genoa; and finally, in about 1590–1610, the center moved to Amsterdam, where the economic center of the European zone remained fixed for almost two centuries.

Between 1780 and 1815 it moved to London, and in 1929 it crossed the Atlantic and became established in New York City.

So Europe's clock chimed the fateful hour on five different occasions, and each time the shift occurred during struggles, clashes, and serious economic crises. In most cases unfavorable economic conditions finally tolled the knell of the old center, which was already in a threatened position, and confirmed the emergence of the new one. Naturally, all of this occurred without any mathematical regularity; a prolonged economic crisis constitutes a test: the strong survive and the weak succumb. Therefore, the center does not collapse every time economic troubles arise. On the contrary, the crises of the seventeenth century generally benefited Amsterdam. During the past few years we have been going through a world crisis of our own that shows every sign of being serious and of long duration. If New York were to succumb—but I don't think it will—the world would have to find or create a new center; if the United States can resist, as seems likely, it may well be even stronger for having stood the test, for the other economies may well suffer more than America as a result of the unfavorable economic situation we are experiencing.

In any event, centering, decentering, and recentering seem on the whole to be linked to prolonged crises in the general economy. Thus, it seems evident that these economic crises must be our point of departure for the difficult study of these mechanisms that turn world history upside down. A close look at one example will enable me to avoid excessive discussion on this point. After a series of avatars, of political accidents, and as a result of the nonconsolidation of the center of the world at Antwerp, the entire Mediterranean had its revenge during the second half of the sixteenth century. Silver was arriving in huge quantities from the American mines. Until then silver had moved along the Atlantic route leading from Spain to Flanders; but after 1568 it began to veer toward the Mediterranean, and Genoa became the center from which it was redistributed. At that point the Mediterranean experienced a sort of economic renaissance, from the Straits of Gibraltar to the Levantine seas. But this "Century of the Genoese," as it has been called, did not last long. The situation deteriorated, and the Genoese fairs of Piacenza, which for almost fifty years had been the great clearing system for European business, no longer played the principal role after 1621. As was to be expected during this post-Discovery period, the Mediterranean once again became a secondary region and remained one for a long time to come.

This decline of the Mediterranean a century after Columbus, and therefore at the end of an enormous and astonishing breathing period, is one of the crucial problems raised by the fat volumes dealing with the Mediterranean space that I published long ago. What date should we assign to this recession—1610, 1620, 1650? Above all, what process should be blamed? This second, more important question has just been answered in a brilliant fashion—and to my mind correctly—in a recent [1975] article by Richard T. Rapp. I do not hesitate to call this one of the finest articles I have read during the past ten years. It proves that after 1570 the Mediterranean world was harassed, bullied, and pillaged by northern ships and merchants, and that these merchants did not make their *initial* fortune in the India companies or in risky ventures on the Seven Seas. They fell upon the wealth present around the Mediterranean and seized it in any way they could, respectable or disreputable. They flooded the area with clever imitations of the excellent southern textiles and even marked them with the universally reputed Venetian seals in order to sell them under that "label" on the usual Venetian markets. As a result, Mediterranean industry lost both its clientele and its reputation. Imagine what would happen if, over a period of twenty, thirty, or forty years, new nations were regularly able to undercut the foreign—and even the domestic—markets of the United States by selling their products under the label "Made in U.S.A." In short, the northerners did not triumph as a result of superior business acumen or

88

the natural process of industrial competition (although the lower salaries in the North were surely a factor); nor was their triumph the fruit of having sided with the Reformation. Their policy was simply to take the place of the former winners, violence being all in the game. Is it necessary to point out that this rule of the game remains in force? The violent division of the world during World War I, which Lenin denounced, was not as new as he thought. Isn't it still a fact of life today? Those who are in the center, or near the center, can lord it over the others.

This leads to my second point: the division of every world-economy into concentric zones, which enjoy increasingly fewer advantages as one moves out from the triumphant pole.

Splendor, wealth, and pleasant living are grouped about the center of the world-economy, at its very heart. There the sunshine of history brings out the bright colors; there high prices, high salaries, banking, luxury merchandise, profitable industries, and capitalist agriculture are evident; and there the point of departure and the point of arrival for long-distance commerce and the afflux of precious metals, respected currency, and letters of credit are to be found. There every precocious form of economic modernity is practiced; the traveler observing fifteenth-century Venice or seventeenth-century Amsterdam or eight-

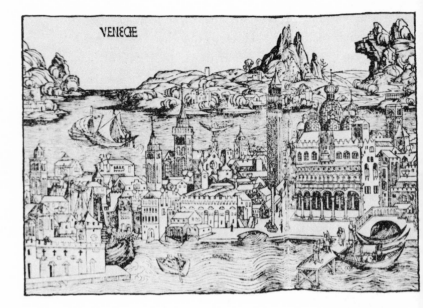

eenth-century London or twentieth-century New York is aware of this. The latest technical skills can usually also be found there, along with the basic scientific knowledge that accompanies them. There "liberties" take root, and although they are not entirely mythical, they are not entirely real, either. Think of what is meant by the "freedom of life in Venice," or the Dutch liberties, or the English ones!

90

This standard of living drops a level when we reach the intermediate countries, those neighbors, rivals, and competitors of the center. There we find few free peasants, few freemen, imperfect exchanges, incomplete banking, financial organizations that are often directed from outside, and relatively traditional industries. Elegant though eighteenth-century France may have appeared, its standard of living was not comparable to England's. John Bull, that overfed meat-eater, wore shoes; but his French counterpart, Jacques Bonhomme, was a puny, wan, and prematurely aged bread-eater with wooden shoes on his feet.

But how far away France seems when we reach the peripheral regions. Take 1650 as an example: the center of the world was tiny Holland, or to be more accurate, Amsterdam. The intermediate or secondary zones were the very active remainder of Europe, that is, the Baltic and North Sea states, England, the Rhine and Elbe regions of Germany, France, Portugal, Spain, and Italy north of Rome. The peripheral regions were Scotland, Ireland, and Scandinavia to the north; plus all of Europe east of a line running from Hamburg to Venice; Italy south of Rome (Naples and Sicily); and lastly beyond the Atlantic, Europeanized America, the periphery *par excellence*. With the exception of Canada and the young English colonies in America, the entire New World was a world based upon slavery. In like manner, the outer reaches of Central Europe, stretching to Poland and beyond, were a zone of *second serfdom*: serfdom, having virtually disappeared there as it had in the West, was reestablished during the sixteenth century.

In short, in 1650 the European world-economy was a juxtaposition, a coexistence of societies that ranged from the already capitalist one of Holland down to those based upon serfdom or slavery, at the very bottom of the ladder. This simultaneity, this synchronism, brings up once more all the problems under discussion. For this layering gives capitalism life: the outer zones feed the intermediate ones and, above all, the center. And what is the center if not the pinnacle, the capitalist superstructure of the whole edifice? Since points of view are reciprocal, if the center depends upon the periphery for supplies, the periphery depends upon the needs of the center that controls it. After all, Western Europe transferred —virtually reinvented—the ancient practice of slavery to the New World and "induced" the new serfdom in Eastern Europe as a result of economic imperatives. This lends weight to Wallerstein's assertion that capitalism is a creation of world inequality; in order to develop, it needed the connivance of the international economy. It was born of the authoritarian organization of a region that was simply too vast. It would not have grown to be as sturdy in a restricted economic area, and it might not have grown at all if cheap labor had not been available.

This theory offers an explanation far different from the usual successive model: slavery, feudalism, capitalism. It proposes a simultaneity, a synchronism so unusual that it must be of great significance. But it does not explain everything; it cannot explain everything. Above all, it cannot explain one point that I believe is essential to the origins of modern capitalism; I am referring to what went on beyond the frontiers of the European world-economy.

Indeed, until the end of the eighteenth century and the appearance of a true world-wide economy, Asia had well-organized and efficient world-economies: China, Japan, the India-Insulinde block, and the world of Islam. It is customary—and accurate—to say that trade relations between these economies and those of Europe were superficial, that they involved only a few luxury articles—pepper, spices, and silks in particular—exchanged for coins, and that it all was of little importance when compared with those economies as a whole. No doubt this is true, but in Europe, as well as in Asia, rich capitalists retained exclusive control over these few supposedly superficial exchanges; this is not, and cannot be, an accident. I have even come to believe that every world-economy is on many occasions manipulated from without. The great historical events of Europe proclaim this insistently,

and no one thinks there is anything wrong in conferring stardom upon Vasco da Gama's arrival at Calcutta in 1498; Cornelis de Houtman's putting into the harbor of the great Javanese city of Bantam in 1595; and Robert Clive's victory at Plassey in 1757, which won Bengal for England. Fate wears seven-league boots. She can take very long steps.

III

I referred to a succession of world-economies in Europe during my discussion of the centers that created and gave life to them, one after the other. It must be pointed out that until about 1750 the dominant centers were always cities, city-states. For Amsterdam, which still dominated the economic world in the mid-eighteenth century, can justifiably be called the last of the city-states, the last *polis* of history. Behind her, the United Provinces were but a shadow government. Amsterdam reigned alone, a brilliant spotlight visible to the entire world, from the Caribbean to the coasts of Japan. However, a new era began toward the middle of the century of the Enlightenment. London, the new sovereign, was not a city-state, but the capital of the British Isles, a position that gave it the irresistible power of a *national market*.

Two phases then: *urban creations and dominions*, and *"national" creations and dominions*. All this will receive only a cursory glance here, not only because these well-known facts are familiar or because I have already discussed them but also because to my mind these familiar facts are only important when taken as a whole, for it is with respect to the whole that the problem of capitalism can be posed and a new light thrown upon it.

95

Until 1750, therefore, Europe rotated about a series of important cities that had been given stardom as a result of the role they played: Venice, Antwerp, Genoa, and Amsterdam. But, in the thirteenth century, no city of that sort yet dominated economic life. This was not because Europe was not yet a structured and organized world-economy. After a period of Moslem domination, the Mediterranean was once again Christian, and Levantine trade offered the West that long-reaching and prestigious antenna without which no world-economy worthy of the name could exist. Two leading regions stood out clearly from the others: Italy to the south and the Netherlands to the north. And the center of gravity of the whole was established midway between the two, in the fairs of Champagne and Brie, fairs that were artificial cities added on to an almost-large city —Troyes—and to three secondary towns—Provins, Bar-sur-Aube, and Lagny. It would be stretching the point to say that this center of gravity was located in a vacuum, for it was not very far from Paris, which at that time was a major commercial center basking in the glory of the reign of Louis IX and the extraordinary fame of its university. Giuseppe Toffanin, historian of humanism, was not blind to this fact in his book, which bears the evocative title *Il secolo senza Roma* [The century without Rome]—in other words, the thirteenth century, the century during which

Rome's cultural sovereignty was usurped by Paris. But it is clear that at that period, the glory of Paris had something to do with the noisy and bustling fairs of Champagne, an international meeting place in almost continuous activity. Woolen cloths and linens from the north—from the Netherlands in the broad sense of the word, a vast nebula of family workshops producing wool, hemp, and linen along the riverbanks from the Marne to the Zuider Zee—were exchanged for the pepper, spices, and currency of Italian merchants and moneylenders. These restricted exchanges of luxury products nevertheless were enough to set in motion an enormous apparatus involving commerce, industries, transports, and credit, and to make these fairs the economic center of Europe of that day.

Champagne declined at the end of the thirteenth century for various reasons: the establishment of a direct maritime link between the Mediterranean and Bruges in 1297, when the sea won out over the land; the improvement of the road running north-south through the German cities via the Simplon and Saint Gotthard passes; and the industrialization of the Italian cities, which were no longer content to dye the ecru woolens imported from the north and now wove their own, giving momentum to the *arte della lana* at Florence. But above all, the serious economic crisis, soon to be joined by the tragedy of the Black Death, played its customary role in the fourteenth century:

Italy, the most powerful partner in the exchanges of Champagne, triumphed during this trial. Italy became, or rather, became once more, the undisputed center of European economic life. All exchanges between north and south came under Italy's control, and in addition, the merchandise reaching Italy from the Far East via the Persian Gulf, the Red Sea, and the caravans of the Levant gave Italy automatic access to all European markets.

Actually, this Italian primacy would for a long time be divided among four powerful cities: Venice, Milan, Florence, and Genoa. It was only after Genoa's defeat in 1382 that Venice's long, but not always tranquil, reign began. It would, however, last for more than a century, as long as Venice dominated the Levantine commercial centers and was the principal redistributor of the sought-after products of the Far East for all of Europe, which hastened to Venice. During the sixteenth century Antwerp supplanted the city of Saint Mark, for it had become the depot for the large quantities of pepper that Portugal imported via the Atlantic, so that the port on the Escaut became an enormous center, dominating Atlantic and northern European commerce. Then, for various political reasons that are too complicated to explain here and that are related to the wars carried on by the Spanish in the Netherlands, the position as dominant city shifted to Genoa. The wealth of the city of Saint

George was based upon trade not with the Levant but with the New World, upon trade with Seville, and upon the floods of silver from the American mines for which Genoa became the European redistributor. Amsterdam finally brought an end to the dispute, and for more than one hundred and fifty years made its preponderance felt from the Baltic to the Levant to the Moluccas. This was essentially owing to its undisputed control over northern merchandise on the one hand and over the "fine spices," such as cinnamon and cloves, on the other, for Amsterdam had quickly grabbed up *all* the Far-Eastern sources of these spices. These quasi-monopolies permitted it to have its way just about everywhere.

But let's leave these city-empires behind and move on to the big problem: national markets and national economies.

A national economy is a political space, transformed by the state as a result of the necessities and innovations of economic life, into a coherent, unified economic space whose combined activities may tend in the same direction. Only England managed this exploit at an early date. In reference to England the term *revolution* recurs: agricultural, political, financial, and industrial revolutions. To this list must be added—giving it whatever name you choose—the revolution that created England's national market.

Otto Hintze, in criticizing Sombart, was one of the first to stress the importance of this transformation, which resulted from the relative abundance of means of transportation within a rather restricted territory: maritime coastal shipping that supplemented the dense network of rivers and canals, and numerous vehicles and pack horses. With London as a go-between, the English shires exchanged and exported their products, especially since England eliminated internal customs duties and tolls at a very early date. In addition, England achieved union with Scotland in 1707, and with Ireland in 1801. One might think that this exploit had already been managed by the United Provinces, but they occupied only a minuscule bit of territory, which was unable to feed its own population. This domestic market had little place in the plans of the Dutch capitalists, who were solely concerned with the foreign market.

France, on the other hand, encountered simply too many obstacles: her economic slowness, her relatively large size, her low per capita income, and difficult communications within her territory. Thus France was too big for the transportation of the day, too diversified, and too unorganized. In his recent and much discussed book, Edward Fox had no trouble showing that there were at least two Frances: a maritime France, lively, flexible, caught up in the economic growth of the eighteenth century and looking exclusively beyond her frontiers, with few connections to the hinterland; and a continental France, land-oriented, conservative, accustomed to her local horizons, and unaware of the economic advantages of international capitalism. This second France consistently controlled political power. Although Paris was the governmental center of France, it was not the economic capital of the territory as a whole; for many years that role was played by Lyons, after the establishment of its fairs in 1461. At the end of the sixteenth century, a shift in favor of Paris seemed imminent, but it never materialized. Only after Samuel Bernard's bankruptcy in 1709 did Paris become the economic center of the French market, and only after the reorganization of the Paris Bourse in 1724 did this market begin to fulfill its role. But by then it was late, and although during the reign of Louis XVI the motor began to race, it did not manage to stimulate and gain control of the whole of French territory.

England's destiny was much simpler. There was only one center—London—which as early as the fifteenth century rapidly assumed the position of economic and political center, all the while shaping the English market to the needs of London, that is, to the advantage of the great local merchants.

In addition, England's insularity helped it to remain independent and to fend off interference from foreign capitalists. Antwerp was faced with a *fait accompli* when Thomas Gresham created the Royal Exchange in 1558. The Hansa cities were faced with a *fait accompli* when the Stalhof was closed in 1597 and the privileges of its former "guests" were repealed. And Amsterdam was faced with a *fait accompli* in the first Navigation Act of 1651. At that time Amsterdam dominated the bulk of European commerce. But England had a means of exerting pressure: given the prevailing wind patterns, Dutch vessels were very often obliged to put into English ports. This may explain why Holland accepted from England protectionist measures that it did not accept from any other country. In any event, England managed to protect its national market and burgeoning industries more successfully than any other European country. Although slow in making itself felt, England's victory over France began early (in my opinion as early as the Treaty of Utrecht of 1713), burst into the open with the treaty negotiated by Eden [Auckland] in 1786, and triumphed in 1815.

With London's accession to power, a page was turned in the history of Europe and of the world, for the establishment of England's economic preponderance, and her consequent preponderance in political leadership, marked the end of an era that had lasted many centuries, an era of city-oriented economies as well as an era of world-economies that, despite

Europe's energy and greed, could not have controlled the rest of the globe from within their confines. What England managed to achieve at Amsterdam's expense did not involve merely repeating past successes; it meant surpassing them.

This conquest of the globe was difficult and was interrupted by incidents and tragic events, but England maintained its preponderance and overcame the obstacles in its path. For the first time the European economy—extending all over the world and shoving aside other economies—aspired to control the economy of the entire world and to be its embodiment all over the globe, where every obstacle collapsed before the Englishman, first of all, and eventually before the European. This held true until 1914. André Siegfried, born in 1875, was twenty-five years old when the twentieth century was born. Much later, in a world bristling with frontier barriers, he recalled with pleasure how he had once gone around the world with only one piece of identification: his calling card! A miracle of the Pax Britannica. Obviously, a certain number of people had to pay the price for this peace.

IV

The English Industrial Revolution, which I have not yet discussed, gave the island's preponderance a new lease on life, a lease drawn up between England and power. But don't worry: I am not going to plunge headlong into this enormous historical problem that in reality continues and besieges us to this very day. Industry still surrounds us on all sides, still revolutionary and still threatening. Don't worry: I am only going to tell you about the beginnings of this enormous movement, and I shall be careful not to get bogged down in the lively controversies in which Anglo-Saxon historians were the first to become engaged, eventually involving other historians as well. Besides, my problem is a restricted one: I want to show to what degree English industrialization fits into the patterns and models I have presented, and to what degree it is a part of the general history of capitalism, which had already witnessed so many sensational developments.

Let me point out that the word *revolution*, here as always, is a misnomer. Etymologically speaking, a revolution is the movement made by a rotating wheel or a revolving planet; a *rapid* movement, once it begins it is sure to stop rather quickly. Yet the Industrial Revolution is a perfect example of a slow movement that was barely noticeable at the beginning. Adam Smith lived in the midst of the first portents of this revolution, yet did not realize it. Doesn't present-day experience reveal that the revolution was very slow, hence difficult, hence complex? Before our very eyes, a part of the Third World is becoming industrialized, but it is encountering unheard-of difficulties and countless failures that appear a priori to be abnormal. In some cases agriculture has not kept up with modernization, or skilled labor is lacking, or the demands of the domestic market are insufficient; on other occasions local capitalists prefer profitable foreign investments to local ones, the state turns out to be wasteful or dishonest, imported technology proves inappropriate or is too costly and affects production costs, exports do not make up for necessary imports, or for one reason or another the international market is hostile, and this hostility has the last word. Now, these avatars are occurring at a time when the revolution has already been invented, when models are available to everyone. A priori, everything should be easy; yet nothing goes well.

Actually, doesn't the situation in all these countries bring to mind what occurred *before* the English experiment, that is, the failure of so many previous revolutions that were potentially realizable insofar as technology was concerned? Ptolemaic Egypt knew about steam power but used it only for amusement. The Roman world had a great body of skills and technology that, in more than one instance, unobtrusively survived through the early Middle Ages and was reemployed during the twelfth and thirteenth centuries. During these centuries of rebirth, Europe increased its energy sources to a fantastic degree and built many water wheels similar to those used in ancient Rome, and windmills too: this already constituted an industrial revolution. China appears to have discovered smelting with coke during the fourteenth century, but this potential revolution was not followed up. In the sixteenth century an entire system of lifting, pumping, and draining water was created for deep mines, but these first modern manufactories, these premature factories, which had involved the investment of a great amount of capital, soon fell victim to the law of diminishing returns. During the seventeenth century the use of charcoal expanded in England, and John U. Nef was justified in calling this the first English industrial revolution, albeit a revolution incapable of spreading and bringing about great upheavals. In France, the signs of industrial progress were clear during the eighteenth century, technological inventions followed one upon the other, and basic science was at least as brilliant there as it was across the Channel. But in the end, England took the decisive steps. Everything seems to have happened there automatically, naturally; and here we have the exciting issue raised by the first industrial revolution in the world, the greatest break in modern history. But why England?

English historians have studied these problems so thoroughly that the non-British historian is easily lost among controversies that he understands separately but that together do nothing at all to simplify the explanation. The only sure thing is that facile and traditional explanations have been pushed aside. There is an increasing tendency to consider the Industrial Revolution as a comprehensive phenomenon, a slow-moving phenomenon, which consequently implies distant and deep-down origins.

When compared with the difficult and chaotic growing pains being experienced by the still-underdeveloped areas of our contemporary world, isn't it all the more astonishing that the "boom" that was part of the English technological revolution, the "boom" that constituted the world's first mass production, was able to develop at the end of the eighteenth century and on into the nineteenth as a fantastic national growth without the motor binding anywhere, without bottlenecks occurring anywhere? The English countryside was drained of its manpower, yet all the while it maintained its productive capacities; the new industrialists found the necessary manpower, skilled and unskilled; the domestic market continued to develop despite rising prices; technology followed close behind and offered its services whenever needed; foreign markets opened one after another, like a chain. And even diminishing profits —for example, the huge drop in the profits of the cotton industry after the first boom—did not result in a crisis. The vast accumulated capital moved else-where, and railroads replaced cotton.

In a word, every sector of the English economy met the demands of this sudden production boom without a bottleneck or a breakdown. Shouldn't this response be attributed to the *entire* national economy? In addition, the cotton revolution in England burgeoned from the lower level, from the level of ordinary life. Its inventions were generally the work of artisans. Industrialists were quite often of humble origin. At the beginning the volume of invested capital, which had been borrowed with little difficulty, was small. It was not London's acquired wealth and her mer-chant and financial capitalism that provoked the astounding mutation; London only gained control of the industry after the 1830s. So we see here admira-bly, and on a wide scale, that what was to be called industrial capitalism was borne up by the strength and vitality of the market economy, and of the underlying economy as well, by the strength and vitality of small and innovative industry, and, no less important, by the entire process of production and exchange. This capitalism could only grow, take shape, and become strong to the degree permitted by the underlying economy.

Nevertheless, the English revolution would cer-tainly not have been what it was without the circumstances that made England at that time the virtually uncontested mistress of the wide world. It is common knowledge that the French Revolution and the Napoleonic wars were largely responsible for this. And if the cotton boom developed over a wide area and continued for a long period, it was because the motor was constantly being refueled by the opening of new markets: the Portuguese and Spanish colonies in the New World, the Turkish Empire, the Indies. The world was an efficient, although unwitting, accomplice of the English Industrial Revolution.

So the rather bitter debate between those who accept only an *internal* explanation for capitalism and for the Industrial Revolution, seeing them as the result of an on-the-spot transformation of socioeconomic structures, and those who consider only an *external* explanation (in other words, the imperialist exploitation of the world)—this debate seems pointless to me. No one can exploit the world simply because he wants to do so. He first must develop his power and consolidate it slowly. But it is certain that, although this power is developed through a slow, internal process, it is strengthened by the exploitation of other parts of the world, and that, in the course of this double process, the chasm separating the exploiter from the exploited constantly deepens. The two explanations—internal and external—are inextricably interwoven.

Here I am, at the end of the puzzle. I am not sure that I have convinced any of my readers along the way. But I am even less sure that I will convince anyone now, as I end my exposition by presenting my view of the world and capitalism today, in the light of yesterday's world and capitalism as I see them and as I have tried to describe them. But shouldn't a historical explanation be valid for the present too? Shouldn't the present corroborate this explanation?

Naturally, it is obvious that capitalism today has changed its size and proportions fantastically. It has expanded in order to remain on the same scale as basic exchanges and financial resources, which have likewise grown fantastically. But, *mutatis mutandis*, I do not think that there has been a complete change in the nature of capitalism from top to bottom.

Three pieces of evidence back me up.

1. Capitalism is still based upon exploiting international resources and opportunities; in other words, it exists on a world-wide scale, or at least it reaches out toward the entire world. Its current major concern is to reconstitute this universalism.

2. Capitalism still obstinately relies upon legal or de facto monopolies, despite the anathemas heaped upon it on this score. As they say today, "organization" keeps circumventing the market. But it is erroneous to believe that this is anything really new.

3. Furthermore, despite what is usually said, capitalism does not overlay the entire economy and all of working society: it never encompasses both of them within one perfect system all its own. The triptych I have described—material life, the market economy, and the capitalist economy—is still an amazingly valid explanation, even though capitalism today has expanded in scope. To become convinced of this one needs only a little inside knowledge about a few present-day activities characteristic of these various levels. At the lowest level, even in Europe, one still finds much self-sufficiency, many services that are not included in the national accounting system, and many shops of artisans. At the middle level, let us take the garment manufacturer: in his production and marketing he is subject to the strict and even ferocious law of competition in which a moment of carelessness or weakness on his part can mean ruin. At the top level I could list, among others, two huge firms, one French and the other German, that I am familiar with, firms that supposedly are competitors—the only competitors in the European market. They do not care which of the two is given an order, for their interests have fused, and the precise way in which these interests are served is of little importance.

Thus, my opinion (an opinion I was very slow to espouse) is confirmed: *capitalism* is the perfect term for designating economic activities that are carried on at the summit, or that are striving for the summit. As a result, large-scale capitalism rests upon the underlying double layer composed of material life and the coherent market economy; it represents the high-profit zone. Thus I have made a superlative of it. I may be criticized for this, but I am not the only one to have held that opinion. In his brochure "Imperialism, the Highest Stage of Capitalism," written in 1917, Lenin asserted that "capitalism is commercial production at its highest level of development" and that "tens of thousands of large businesses are everything, millions of small ones are nothing." But this self-evident truth of 1917 was an old, a very old, truth. Journalists, economists, and sociologists often fail to take historical dimensions and perspectives into account in their writings. And don't many historians do the very same thing, as if the period they study existed in a vacuum, or was both a beginning and an end? Thus Lenin, who had a perspicacious turn of mind, wrote in this same brochure: "Old capitalism, where free competition reigned, was characterized by the exportation of merchandise. Present-day capitalism, in which monopolies reign supreme, is characterized by the exportation of capital." These assertions are more than debatable: capitalism has always been monopolistic, and merchandise and capital have always circulated simultaneously, for capital and credit have always been the surest way of capturing and

113

controlling a foreign market. Long before the twentieth century the exportation of capital was a fact of daily life, for Florence as early as the thirteenth century, and for Augsburg, Antwerp, and Genoa during the sixteenth century. During the eighteenth century capital flowed through Europe and the world. Need I observe that all the methods, dealings, and tricks of the financial world were not born in 1900 or in 1914? Capitalism was familiar with them all, and, yesterday as today, its uniqueness and its strength lie in its ability to move from one trick to another, from one way of doing things to another, to change its plans ten times as the economic conjunctures dictate—and, as a result, to remain relatively faithful, relatively consistent with itself.

What I personally regret, not so much as a historian but as a man of my time, is the refusal in both the capitalist world and the socialist world to draw a distinction between capitalism and the market economy. To those in the West who attack the misdeeds of capitalism, politicians and economists reply that these wrongdoings are a lesser evil, the indispensable reverse side of the free-enterprise-and-market-economy coin. I do not believe that. To those who, as part of a movement of ideas that is noticeable even in the U.S.S.R., worry about the ponderousness of the socialist economy and would like it to be more "spontaneous" (I construe that word to mean "more free''), the reply is that this lack of spontaneity is a lesser evil, the indispensable reverse side of the destruction-of-the-capitalist-scourge coin. I do not believe that either. But is my concept of the ideal society realizable? In any event, I don't think it has many partisans around the globe.

CODA

I would have ended my exposition here, had I not one final bit of advice to pass on as a historian.

History is always being begun anew; it is always working itself out, striving to surpass itself. Its fate is shared by all the social sciences. So I do not believe that the history books I am writing will be valid for decades to come. No book is ever written once and for all, and we all know it.

My interpretation of capitalism and the economy is based upon many hours spent in archives and many hours spent pouring over books, but in the end the statistical data are inadequate and do not mesh sufficiently; we are forced to work more with qualitative than with quantitative information. Monographs providing production curves, profit rates, and investment rates, and those providing careful balance sheets for business, or even an approximate estimate of the attrition of fixed capital, are extremely scarce. In vain I have sought from colleagues and friends for more precise information on these various questions. But I have met with little success.

I believe, however, that precisely this type of approach may provide a way out of the explanations that, for want of anything better, I have proposed. Breaking down the problem in order to understand it more fully, dividing it into three levels or stages, amounts to mutilating and manipulating a much more complex economic and social reality. In truth, we must grasp the whole in order to grasp at the same time the reasons for the change in growth rates that appeared simultaneously with mechanization. As far as the economic history of the past is concerned, a total, global history would be possible if we could succeed in applying the modern methods of a sort of national accounting, a kind of macroeconomy. I would set the following tasks before young historians: to follow the changes in national revenues, the national per capita income; to reevaluate René Baehrel's pioneer work on Provence in the seventeenth and eighteenth centuries; to try to determine the correlations between "budget and national revenue," as was done at the 1976 colloquium at Prato, Italy; or to attempt to measure the discrepancy, which differs for each period, between the gross product and the net product, following the advice of Simon Kuznets, whose hypotheses on this question seem to me of prime importance to a comprehension of modern growth. In my books I have now and then opened a window onto landscapes that are but dimly visible; but one window is not enough. A coordinated, if not a collective, study is indispensable.

Of course, that does not mean that tomorrow's history will be economic history *ne varietur*. Economic accounting at the best is nothing but a study of flow, of variations in national income; it is not a measurement of the mass of patrimonies, of national wealth. However, this mass is also accessible and must be studied. For historians, for all other social scientists, and for all objective scientists, there will always be a new America to discover.

Sources of Illustrations

Page 13: "Schnittermahl, Herbstsaat, und Flachshecheln" ["Cutting, Fall Sowing, and Carding of Flax"]. Woodcut by Petrus de Crescentiis, Frankfurt, 1538. Reprinted from Friedrich Zoepfl, *Deutsche Kulturgeschichte*, vol. 2, *Vom. 16. Jahrhundert bis Gegenwart* (Frieburg im Breisgau: Herder & Co., 1930).

Page 18: "Tailor's Workshop," by Jobst Amman, 1568. Reprinted from Friedrich Zoepfl, *Deutsche Kulturgeschichte*, vol. 2, *Vom. 16. Jahrhundert bis Gegenwart* (Freiburg im Breisgau: Herder & Co., 1930).

Page 29: Woodcut of Florentine market workers, *Contrasto di Cornevale e Quaresima*. Reprinted from *The Horizon Book of the Renaissance*, by the editors of *Horizon Magazine* (New York: American Heritage Publishing Co., 1961), by permission of the Bibliotheca Riccardiana, Florence.

Page 48: Interior of a bank. Woodcut from *Il Libro di Mercantie*, Florence, 1490. Reprinted from Arnold Toynbee, ed., *Cities of Destiny* (New York: McGraw-Hill Book Co., 1967).

Page 55: Peddlers at the foot of the column of Arcadius at the Avret-pazari. Reprinted from Halil Inalcik, *The Ottoman Empire: The Classical Age, 1300–1600*, trans. Norman Itzkowitz and Colin Imber (London: Weidenfeld and Nicolson, 1973), by permission of the Museo Civico Correr, Venice.

Page 66: Title page from Jan Ympijn, *Nieuwe instructie ende bewijs der looffelijcker Consten des Rekenboecks, ende Rekeninghe te houdene nae die Italiaensche maniere* . . . (Antwerp, 1543). Reprinted from Leon Voet, *Antwerp, The Golden Age: The Rise and Glory of the Metropolis in the Sixteenth Century* (Antwerp: Mercatorfonds, 1973), by permission of the Antwerp Stadsbibliotheek.

Page 90: "Venice." Woodcut in Hartmann Schedel's so-called *Nuremberg Chronicle*, Nuremberg (Koberger), 1493. Reprinted from A. Hyatt Mayor, *Prints and People: A Social History of Printed Pictures* (New York: Metropolitan Museum of Art, 1971), by permission of the Metropolitan Museum of Art.

Page 94: "The Isle of Amboina." Reprinted from *A Collection of Voyages and Travels, Some Now first Printed from Original Manuscripts, Others Now first Published in English*, 3d ed., 6 vols. (London, 1744), 2: 162.

Page 103: "The Royal Exchange." Interior, facing west. Etching by Wenceslaus Hollar, London, 1644. Reprinted from Arthur M. Hind, *Wenceslaus Hollar and His Views of London and Windsor in the Seventeenth Century* (London: John Land, The Bodley Head Ltd., 1922), pl. 32.

Library of Congress Cataloging in Publication Data

Braudel, Fernand.
    Afterthoughts on material civilization and capitalism.

    (The Johns Hopkins symposia in comparative history)
    Lectures presented at Johns Hopkins University. Apr. 1976.
    1. Economic history—Addresses, essays, lectures. 2. Capitalism
—Addresses, essays, lectures. I. Title. II. Series. III. Title: Material
civilization and capitalism.
HC45.B6913   330.12′2′09   76-47368
ISBN 0-8018-1901-6 (hardcover)
ISBN 0-8018-2217-3 (paperback)